Flagstaff Public Library
Arizona Collection

THE
WILD WEST

THE
WILD
WEST

HISTORY, MYTH & THE
MAKING OF AMERICA

Frederick Nolan

FREDERICK NOLAN

CHARTWELL
BOOKS, INC.

To my son, Christian, who did not live to read it.

Published by
CHARTWELL BOOKS, INC.
A Division of BOOK SALES, INC.
114 Northfield Avenue
Edison, New Jersey 08837

First published by Arcturus Publishing Limited

This edition published 2004

British Library Cataloguing-in-Publication Data: a catalogue
record for this book is available from the British Library

© Arcturus Publishing Limited
26/27 Bickels Yard, 151–153 Bermondsey Street, London SE1 3HA

ISBN 0-7858-1857-X

Edited by Paul Whittle
Cover & book design by Alex Ingr
Cover Image: *Day of the Dons Festival* by Patricia Doolittle, CA, USA
©2000 P. Doolittle/www.artby2west.com
Reprinted with kind permission of the artist

Printed in China

CONTENTS

'THE WHITE MEN MADE US MANY PROMISES, MORE THAN I CAN REMEMBER, BUT THEY NEVER KEPT BUT ONE: THEY PROMISED TO TAKE OUR LAND, AND THEY TOOK IT.'

Chief Red Cloud of the Oglala Sioux (1822–1909)

INTRODUCTION

'Go West, young man, and grow up with the country.'
Horace Greeley (1811–1872), US politician and journalist

THE HISTORY OF THE AMERICAN WEST – and by that is meant exclusively the trans-Mississippi West – is, largely, the story of the coming to nationhood of the United States of America. In 1803, when Thomas Jefferson negotiated the purchase of the 820,000 square miles of French-owned land called Louisiana for eighty million francs ($15,000,000) and increased the national territory by 140 per cent, America was a relatively small republic (try to imagine the map without Missouri, Nebraska, Iowa, Arkansas, North and South Dakota, Kansas, Minnesota, Montana, Wyoming, most of Louisiana and parts of Oklahoma and Colorado on it). In the census of 1800, the country's total population was 5,308,483, a figure which included nearly a million slaves. The centre of population was just eighteen miles southwest of Baltimore, Maryland, and the 'far western frontier' was the Mississippi River with America's pioneer Indiana Territory on its eastern side and unexplored Louisiana on the western. In the century that followed the United States experienced another revolution far more significant than the earlier one, metamorphosing from what had been a largely colonial squirearchy to a mighty nation stretching 'from sea to shining sea'. At the end of that hundred years its population had multiplied fourteenfold to 75,994,575. The centre of population had moved west to a point six miles south of Columbus, Indiana and the once empty prairies and mountains were dotted with new cities and towns: Chicago, Milwaukee, St Louis, Kansas City, Denver, Omaha, Seattle, Salt Lake, Phoenix. Railroads linked east and west. The 'frontier' no longer existed.

To set down accurately and comprehensively the whole and complete history of that extraordinary transformation would require a book far bigger than this one, indeed perhaps a series of books. That does not mean, however, that a single book cannot, or should not, endeavour to serve as an introduction to the people, the events, the adventure, and the drama of the irresistible surge of American – and European – emigration toward the setting sun. It is not necessary to eat the whole beast to find out what buffalo tastes like.

Although some lesser-known events and a few unsung heroes (and heroines) of the moving frontier are included here, it is possible that too much emphasis has been given to personalities who have perhaps already received more attention than they really merit. However, there is a reason for that. Readers coming to the subject for the first time – and it is mostly for them that this book has been written – are more often prompted to do so by a desire to learn whether events they have heard about or seen portrayed in movies have any basis in fact, than any particular hunger to know (for instance) what yield of calves the average cattle rancher could expect in a good season.

However, whether Wild Bill Hickok, who is included, is a more relevant choice than (say) gun manufacturer Samuel Colt, who is not, whether the Sioux leader Crazy Horse should be given more space than (say) railroad baron Leland Stanford, it is impossible to say. What historian would be bold enough to contend that the machinations of politicians in Washington which led to the Indian Wars were a more potent factor in the history of the West than the determination and courage of the officers and men of the US Army who fought them? Or that Billy the Kid was a less (or more) significant historical figure than President Rutherford B. Hayes, who held office during the Kid's lifetime?

The history of the West is a vast, rich mosaic made of more parts than can be counted, and not all of them are exciting. Indeed some of them, although worthy, are inescapably dull: the exhausting daily grind of a sod house homesteader living on the Kansas prairie, the steamy drudgery of an anonymous Chinese laundryman, the sad duties of some forgotten undertaker, to name but a few aspects of the West little talked about. Nevertheless, all of them were an integral part of the picture. That this book excludes such stories does not mean they were unimportant – only that it is simply not possible to include them all. So if famous names like that of 'Buffalo Bill' Cody – a man who quite probably did more to make the world aware of the West than any other human being – appear only briefly, the same rule applies. No book, no film, no television series can ever encompass the whole story.

The West, as the Kiowa poet L. Scott Momaday said, is a dream. Not just one man's dream: it was and it is everybody's dream. In these pages are some of the people who made that dream come true – soldiers and missionaries, outlaws and storekeepers, soldiers' wives and soiled doves, British; French; Germans; Swedes; some brave, others fools, some legends, some forgotten – who played their part, noble or otherwise, in opening the American frontier.

CHAPTER ONE

TRAILBLAZERS

O N 30 APRIL, 1803, and for a mere $15 million, President Thomas Jefferson – who had begun negotiations seeking only to buy the port of New Orleans – doubled the size of the infant United States by concluding with the Emperor Napoleon the purchase of over 800,000 square miles (1,300,000 sq km) of mostly unexplored French-owned land in central North America bounded on the west by Spanish California and known as Louisiana. The first priority, the President decided, was to find out exactly what lay out there beyond the 'frontier' and he persuaded Congress to finance a voyage of expedition which would establish whether there was a route across this vast and unknown country to the Pacific.

At this time the Missouri River had been charted only as far as the villages of the Mandan Indians in the Dakota region. What lay between there and the Pacific coast, or how far one was from the other, no white man knew. Some believed there were mountains made entirely of salt; others that California was an island. Stories abounded of strange tribes living in the wilderness: man-hating Amazon women who cut off their right breasts so they would not get in the way of their bowstrings, a tribe of Welsh-speaking Indians descended from a man who had reached America before Columbus,

American explorers Meriwether Lewis (1774–1809) and William Clark (1770–1838) at the mouth of the Columbia River during their exploration of the Louisiana Territory. Painting by Frederic Remington (1861–1909).

and a community of 18-inch-high devils in human form. Some Americans believed that America's Indians might be descendants of the lost tribes of Israel.

The man Jefferson chose to establish what was legend and what was fact was his thirty-year-old personal secretary, soldier and scholar Captain Meriwether Lewis. He in turn selected as his co-leader William Clark, a younger brother of the famous soldier and frontiersman George Rogers Clark who had conquered the country west of the Allegheny mountains during the American Revolution. They were to prove a good team: throughout the expedition Lewis's better education and scientific training were perfectly comple-mented by Clark's practical ability and understanding of frontier survival, and there was never a single incidence of tension or rivalry between them.

They left Wood River, near the mouth of the Missouri River, on 14 May, 1804 in two pirogues (a long narrow canoe made from a single tree trunk) and a 60ft keelboat – a large flat freight barge, pulled by horses or by hand. They travelled up the Missouri, reaching the villages of the Mandan Indians at the mouth of the Knife River in what is now North Dakota on 26 October, where they spent the winter and where the only man to perish on the journey, Clark's servant Charles Floyd, died of peritonitis.

They resumed their journey in April, the party now reduced to thirty-three men – and one woman. This was a Shoshone named Sacajawea ('Bird Woman') who was married to a member of the expedition, Toussant Charbonneau, and hugely pregnant at this time. Lewis decided to take her along with him and she became an inestimable asset to the expedition, acting as their interpreter and intermediary with the various tribes of Indians they encountered on their journey. Lewis, who called her 'Jenny' and Clark, who called her 'Janey' both spoke very highly of her talents, and Clark, in particular, was much taken by Sacajawea's infant son, to whom he gave the nickname Pompey, meaning headman.

The Corps of Discovery – the 'official' name of the expedition – made every effort to meet peacefully with the more than fifty tribes of Indians they encountered, to try to understand their customs and to cement cordial relations between them and the Great White Father, as they described the President, by presenting their leaders with presents – coloured beads, calico shirts, mirrors, bells, needles, ribbons, kettles and rings – and where apposite, special 'peace tokens' struck by Jefferson for just this purpose. In this mission they would prove so successful that a number of Indian delegations went east to meet Jefferson even before Lewis and Clark had themselves returned.

The expedition reached the Great Falls of the Missouri in present-day Montana in June, crossed the Stony (Rocky) Mountains, and descended the Columbia River to the Oregon Territory and the Pacific Ocean, which they reached 7 November, 1805. This time there were no friendly Indians to shelter them, and unable to find any ships to take them back East, they built Fort Clatsop and endured a dreadful winter there.

They started their return journey on 23 March, 1806, then split up, with Clark leading an exploration of the Yellowstone guided by Sacajawea, while Lewis led a party of nine men over the Rockies via what is now called Lewis and Clark Pass and reached the upper Missouri on 11 July. While awaiting the arrival of Clark, Lewis took three men to explore the Marias River (named for his cousin, Maria Wood). It was here the only serious clash with native Americans took place, when two Blackfeet were killed, one by Lewis himself, as they tried to steal horses and weapons from Lewis's camp; he then hurried to his rendezvous with Clark, fearful that a larger party of Blackfeet might come after them. None did, although a side effect of this encounter was that the Blackfeet remained hostile toward the white man for many years. Just a few days later, on 12 August, Clark rejoined Lewis near the mouth of the Yellowstone only to find that the preceding day the younger man had been shot through both thighs by Pierre Cruzat, who had mistaken him for an elk.

Although he had to be carried on a litter for some time, Lewis's wound healed within a month, by which time they were pushing back down the Missouri, reaching St Louis on 23 September, 1806, after an absence of two years, four months and nine days. They had covered 7,689 punishing miles [12,302 km], and brought back with them countless specimens of hitherto unknown plants and wildlife, as well as journals bulging with geographic and topographical information. The Lewis and Clark expedition, originally budgetted at $2,500 (though in the end the actual cost was $38,722.25) was and remains probably the most significant exploration ever accomplished in the history of the United States until men landed on the moon.

Later, President Thomas Jefferson appointed Meriwether Lewis governor of Louisiana Territory, that country through which he had just travelled, while William Clark, who resigned from the army in February, 1807, was made Louisiana's Brigadier General of Militia and principal Indian agent. Lewis died in mysterious circumstances – possibly suicide, maybe murder – in 1809. In 1813 Clark was named governor of the Missouri Territory and lived long enough to serve under five Presidents; he died full of honours at St Louis on 1 September, 1838. He persuaded the Shoshone woman Sacajawea, who had remained at the Mandan villages with her husband Charbonneau, to come to St Louis and, according to one story, they left their son Jean Baptiste with Clark to be educated. Later, a daughter Lizette also reached St. Louis and Clark became her guardian, too. Many historians believe Sacajawea died in 1812, while others contend that she lived among her people in Wyoming until she was about one hundred years old and died on 9 April, 1884. Whichever is true, there are many monuments to her at places related to her life.

Almost in the footsteps of Lewis and Clark came a hardy breed of explorers and frontiersmen who ventured fearlessly into the unexplored wilderness, blazing trails that within a few short decades would be utilized by first a trickle, then a flood of emigrants heading west in search of new lands and new lives. Indeed, before Lewis and Clark returned, the United States Army had launched a twenty-man expedition led by Lt Zebulon Pike to locate the source of the Mississippi River. Despite its commander's debatable conclusions, the following year a second expedition, again led by Pike, set out to explore and map the Southwest, traversing the future States of Kansas, southern Nebraska, and New Mexico, and travelling as far south as Mexico City.

Meanwhile a new industry – the fur trade – blossomed. Europeans had been buying American furs since the sixteenth century, when the French had controlled and capitalized upon the trade. After them came the English and the Dutch and then at the beginning of the nineteenth century a new breed of entrepreneurs, men like John Jacob Astor, Manuel Lisa and Pierre Chouteau, who set out to challenge the former dominance of British and French organizations like the Hudson's Bay Company and the North West Company.

In 1807 Manuel Lisa loaded sixty men into keelboats and headed up the Missouri and on as far as the point where the Big Horn River meets the Yellowstone, where he built a fort and trading post, with another sited at the three forks of the Missouri. Just as the British had earlier made the Blackfeet dependent upon them for trade goods, guns and whiskey, so now did Lisa's Missouri Fur Company involve the Crow Indians, thus laying the foundations for a bloody conflict of long duration. In 1810 an expedition financed by Astor sailed around the Horn in the brig Tonquin to establish his American Fur Company at Fort Astoria in what is now Oregon. The venture proved unsuccessful, but the die was cast: the opening of the West had begun.

Then a second war –'the War of 1812' with Britain which lasted until 1815 – put a temporary stop to further government exploration of the Louisiana Territory and it was not until 1819 that Major Stephen Long led an expedition to explore the territory south of the Missouri region. He returned so unimpressed that he dubbed the country he had explored 'the Great American Desert'. This myth was largely to persist until after the Civil War of 1861-65.

Others were shrewder and knew better. On 7 July 1822, trader William Becknell had blazed an 800 mile (1,300 km) trail to Spanish Santa Fe with three wagons loaded with merchandise, and in the same year William Henry Ashley and Andrew Henry set up the Rocky Mountain Fur Company which would dominate the industry for a decade until it was superseded by Astor's American Fur Company. Just two years later, mountain men Jedediah Smith and William Sublette rediscovered South Pass, which would become the most-used route for crossing the mountains by guides taking emigrant trains west, the earliest entrepreneurs of mass travel.

Probably no advertisement ever printed had such far-reaching effects upon the history and exploration of the American West as the one which appeared in the St Louis newspapers on 13 February, 1822:

TO ENTERPRISING YOUNG MEN

The subscriber wishes to engage ONE HUNDRED MEN, *to ascend the river Missouri to its source, there to be employed for one, two, or three years. For particulars enquire of Major Andrew Henry, near the Lead Mines, in the County of Washington (who will ascend with, and command the party) or to the subscriber at St Louis.*

Wm. H. Ashley

It was with this 1822 invitation to adventure that the fur trade got fully into its stride, when the first boatload of Ashley's trappers – among them an 18-year old blacksmith's apprentice named Jim Bridger, tall, serious-minded 23-year-old Jedediah Smith, riverboat man Mike Fink, Thomas Fitzpatrick, William Sublette, and Hugh Glass – headed up the Missouri towards what they called 'the shining mountains.' Out in the wilderness these 'company men' and others, rugged individualists all, would hunt, trap and skin the countless beaver and other fur-bearing animals which flourished in the virgin forests, then bring their bounty out of the mountains to a pre-arranged meeting with the fur traders. In the summer of 1825 something like 120 of them appeared in the foothills of the Uintah Mountains of Utah to trade their catches for money, supplies – and whiskey – the first 'rendezvous.' For the next three decades the fur trade would rule the West.

JIM BRIDGER,
KING OF THE MOUNTAIN MEN

Born in Virginia, Jim Bridger was apprenticed to a St. Louis blacksmith at the age of fourteen; once he left for the mountains it was seventeen years before he came back. He was in the party which abandoned Hugh Glass in 1823; the following year he discovered the Great Salt Lake, which he at first believed was the Pacific Ocean. Bridger's descriptions of his discoveries – such as the geysers at what is now Yellowstone Park – were often at first disbelieved ('They said I was the damnedest liar ever lived,' he complained); as a result he took pleasure in telling 'tall stories' about his exploits to gullible listeners. In 1830 he became one of the organizers of the Rocky Mountain Fur Company, trapping in Blackfoot country and participating in the battle with warriors of that tribe at Pierre's Hole on 18 July 1832. Although, like Kit Carson, he was illiterate, Bridger was a shrewd judge of character. When the Rocky Mountain Fur Company was dissolved in 1834 he teamed up with Tom Fitzpatrick and Milton Sublette. The following winter he was back in Blackfoot country with Joe Meek and Carson, and married a Flathead Indian woman with whom he had several children.

In 1838 Bridger joined the American Fur Company and with Louis Vasquez began construction of a fort named after himself in Wyoming. This became one of the principal trading posts on the Oregon Trail, a military post and a Pony Express station. When his first wife died, Bridger married a woman of the Ute tribe and fathered two more children. Unable to read, he hired a boy to read Shakespeare aloud, and often quoted the Bard.

Ousted from Fort Bridger by the Mormons in 1853, he guided Gen. Albert Sidney Johnston's column to Salt Lake City during the so-called Mormon War of 1857–8. After guiding Reynolds' Yellowstone Expedition (1859–60), Berthoud's engineering party (1861) and the ill-fated Powder River expedition (1865–6), Bridger settled near Westport, Missouri, where he later bought a farm. His health began to fail, and in 1873 he went blind. He died on 17 July 1878, just three days after Sheriff Pat Garrett killed Billy the Kid at Fort Sumner, New Mexico. A common man in the very best sense, he was one of the most able, best liked and best known of all the mountain men.

The earliest 'mountain men' or 'voyageurs,' as they sometimes called themselves, had been first drawn to the virgin forests and rivers as trappers and traders. Initially there were just a few, independently trapping beaver, otter, mink and marten in what are now Colorado and Wyoming, long before the 'companies' were formed. Men like 'Old Bill' Williams, Jim Beckwourth and the legendary 'Liver Eating' Johnson went year after year into the wilderness to find new trapping rivers and fresh hunting grounds. Many of them never came back: only the toughest survived. The story of one of them, John Colter, graphically illustrates how tough it was.

Colter was a loner. He was out in the wilderness trapping furs long before Lewis and Clark's expedition found its way to the mountains. In his search for furs, Colter was the first man to see what is now Yellowstone Park, but no one would believe his stories of steaming hot springs and geysers spouting a hundred feet into the air. In 1808 he and another trapper, John Potts, strayed too far into Blackfoot territory and were surrounded by some five hundred Indians. Colter surrendered but his partner kept fighting, killing one of their leaders. The Blackfeet in turn killed Potts, disembowelling him and then throwing his entrails, lungs and heart into Colter's face. Then one of the Indian leaders asked Colter how fast he could run. Knowing the way their minds worked, Colter told them he was as slow as a snail, whereupon they stripped him naked, gave him a thirty second start and told him to run for his life. Thorny bushes, sharp flints, rocks tearing at his unprotected skin and bare feet, Colter did just that, heading for the Madison River, five or six miles away, with the Blackfeet screaming behind him intent on cutting him to bits. After three or four miles he had outrun all but one warrior, who he tripped and killed with his own lance, then concealed himself from the others by plunging into the icy river and hiding under a pile of driftwood until they gave up looking for him.

When they were gone, he swam down the river for another four or five miles and then started running again. Ten days and two hundred and fifty miles (400 km) later, starving and dehydrated, his feet torn and bloody, his skin blistered from the sun and full of festering thorns, he reached Lisa's Bighorn River fort. Amazingly, after only a short time to recuperate, he put together another outfit and went back to the mountains trapping and – if the opportunity occurred – ambushing Blackfeet. It's said that after another equally harrowing 1810 encounter with the Indians in which several of his friends were killed, Colter swore to quit trapping and 'be damned if I ever come into it again.' He returned to St. Louis, where he became a neighbour of frontiersman Daniel Boone, got married and had a son. He died in 1813, aged about thirty-nine.

Tough as Colter was, there were mountain men even tougher. Such a one was Hugh Glass. No one knows where he was born or who his parents were – some say he might have been of Irish descent – nor anything about his early life, other than that he might have been a pirate in the Gulf of Mexico with Jean Lafitte (and then again, maybe not). What is known for sure is that he was reckless and insubordinate, rugged and self-reliant, and that in 1823 he joined an expedition up the Missouri led by William H. Ashley, organizer of the rendezvous system.

Wounded in a battle with Arikara Indians – 'Rees' as they were known – he recovered in time to be one of a party sent to relieve a group of hunters left at Fort Henry, at the mouth of the Yellowstone River. Late in August, 1823, Glass was attacked and severely mauled by a grizzly bear, so badly that it seemed impossible he could live. Ashley knew he and his men could not safely remain much longer in the land of the hostile and dangerous Arikara, and asked for two volunteers to stay with the dying man until the end. John Fitzgerald and young Jim Bridger stepped forward.

They stayed with Glass until he died, or until they thought he was dead, then took his rifle, his ammunition and his other possessions, loaded them into their own packs and left. But Hugh Glass was not dead. He regained consciousness to find himself totally alone in the wilderness. Fortunately for him there was water in a nearby spring and berries on the trees he could eat, and ten days later he was ready to begin what would become an epic journey. Racked by pain and fever, passing in and out of consciousness, he set out for the only place in that wilderness where he could get help, Fort Kiowa, half the breadth and then half the length of South Dakota away.

According to legend, he got lucky and happened upon a buffalo calf that just had been brought down by wolves. He drove the wolves off by setting fire to the grass, and remained by the carcass, gorging on buffalo meat, until his wounds began to heal. Then he moved on, crawling maybe a mile a day, sometimes two or three as his strength grew. Living on roots, berries, carrion, whatever he could find, he crawled, staggered, limped an incredible three hundred miles [480 km] down the Grand River toward the Missouri. There, they say, he was befriended by Sioux Indians who took him the rest of the way to Fort Kiowa.

No one now knows all the facts, but that it happened is not in question. Astonishingly, the adventures of Hugh Glass were anything but over. Now fully recovered, he determined to go back up the river and avenge himself upon Jim Bridger and John Fitzgerald, the two men who had abandoned him. He joined up with a small party going north to the Mandan villages; they were attacked by a large band of Rees and all the traders were killed except for Glass and Toussaint Charbonneau, the husband of Sacajawea.

Glass continued north to Fort Henry, only to find it had been abandoned; a scrawled note on the gate told him Ashley's new headquarters were in the Big Horn country of Montana. On he went until he reached his destination and there found Jim Bridger, who was understandably terrified by this apparent return from the dead. After hearing Jim's side of things, Glass forgave Jim because of his youth and set out grimly to find the faithless Fitzgerald, half a continent away.

Heading south, having one narrow escape after another (and again being reported dead when he was not) he eventually located

Fitzgerald, who had enlisted in the US Army, at Fort Atkinson near what is now Omaha, Nebraska. There, the legend says, 'To the man he addressed himself as he did to the boy [Bridger] – 'Go, false man and answer to your own conscience and to your God; I have suffered enough in all reason by your perfidy.'

Repossessing his rifle from Fitzgerald, Glass rode off to the Southwest, where he later traded around Santa Fe and trapped in the Ute country. He was yet again dangerously wounded, this time by an Indian arrow; yet again he survived and returned to the Yellowstone River country. In the winter of 1832–33 his old enemies the Rees – and Fate – caught up with him, killing and scalping Glass and two companions as they were crossing the frozen river. It was the end of a legend and, in a way, the beginning of the end of the era of the mountain men.

By the time Hugh Glass died, the fur trade was already past its zenith and ten years later it was gone. The mountain men now became scouts, pathfinders for the military expeditions which were being sent with increasing frequency to map and quantify the new lands, or for the growing numbers of emigrant parties setting out for the western territories. Among the most notable of these was Joseph Reddeford Walker, an unsung pathfinder who opened up huge new areas of the unexplored continent.

Born in Tennessee in 1798, Walker moved with his family to Missouri in 1819, and accompanied a party of hunters and trappers to New Mexico a year or two later. After helping to chart and mark the Santa Fe trail, he served briefly as the Sheriff of Independence, Missouri, a town he is said to have named. In February, 1831 he set forth on a trading expedition in Cherokee country, where he met Captain Benjamin Bonneville, an army officer who was planning a fur trading operation in the Rockies financed by wealthy New York businessmen.

in 1861 organized the group that would open up central Arizona. He was throughout his life a man whose 'chief delight was to explore unknown regions.' When he died in 1872, it must have given him considerable satisfaction to know that it was largely over trails he had discovered that Americans flooded into the country and made it, in 1850, the state of California.

CHAPTER TWO

THE WAY WEST

AS THE ARMY BEGAN building roads into the new territories, and then added strategically-sited forts to protect them, the stream of emigrants moving west began to grow, its numbers swollen by thousands of Europeans fleeing revolution and upheaval seeking new hope and a new future in America. Once the main trails west were well and truly blazed that stream became an unstoppable torrent of emigration that would continue unabated for another forty years.

By the late 1820s riverboats were pushing ever further up the navigable rivers, wagons were regularly plying the route originally blazed by William Becknell from Independence, Missouri to Santa Fé in New Mexico, where commerce had boomed following the discovery of gold near Taos (and where, incidentally, one of the miners was John Sutter, who later relocated to California). In 1832 Nathaniel Wyeth led the first wagon train across the plains to the Pacific Northwest, following the trace charted by Jedediah Smith that became known as The Oregon Trail.

Oregon was not the only destination. In the middle 1820s emigrants also flooded south from Virginia, the Carolinas and Kentucky into Texas, then part of Coahuila, Mexico. Expansion on this scale was not always achieved peacefully. From the start the newcomers

Remember the Alamo! Mexican general Santa Anna mounts the final assault on the beleaguered defenders of the Alamo, 6 March 1836. The battle made Jim Bowie and Davy Crockett into household names, and fanned the flames of Texan independence.

to Texas had little in common with the resident Mexican population, and by 1830 they outnumbered it three-to-one. Worse, they ignored the requirement that they observe the Catholic faith and worse again, refused to pay taxes. These differences came to a head when the Mexican government passed a whole new set of laws designed to discourage further immigration and stationed troops all over Texas to enforce them. The Texans refused to accept Mexican authority and little by little moved towards rebellion and, ultimately, independence.

THE BATTLE OF THE ALAMO

The fire of Texian (this was the contemporary usage) rebellion was lit when General Antonio Lopez de Santa Anna Perez de Labron, the President (read dictator) of Mexico, passed laws ordering the Texians to surrender their firearms to the military. In the course of enforcing this policy, Colonel Ugartechea, commandant of the garrison at San Antonio de Bexar, sent a company of soldiers, under command of Captain Castañeda, to the little town of Gonzales to reclaim an old six-pounder cannon which had been loaned to the townspeople by the military as a defence against Indians. When they arrived, they were greeted by the muzzle of the fully primed cannon, over which had been erected a banner that declaring: 'Come and get it!'

When Castañeda reported this defiance, Santa Anna immediately sent an army commanded by his brother-in-law General Martin Perfecto de Cos to 'finish off' these Texian troublemakers. The Texians responded by forming a volunteer army, and elected Stephen F. Austin as its commander-in-chief. Shortly afterwards Austin was replaced by ex-Indian fighter Colonel Edward Burleson, who led his untrained volunteers to San Antonio and laid siege to the town.

The weather was bad, with continuous rain; there wasn't enough food, and little clothing. The independently-minded volunteers began to talk about going home – there seemed no likelihood of any real fighting, and they could soon get back if there was. Fortunately, before the Army fell apart, the provisional government offered the volunteers pay of $20 per month to stay on, and they stayed, although there was still indecision and dissension. Then two Americans, Sam Maverick and John Smith, escaped from the town and reported that General Cos' troops were starving, low on ammunition, and in poor spirits.

At this juncture, Ben Milam joined them. Ben was all that a leader should be; brave, daring, handsome, an Indian fighter, veteran of both the War of 1812 and the Revolutionary War. He took the bull by the horns. 'Who will come with Old Ben Milam into San Antone?' he roared, and 250 men jumped to go with him. They attacked at dawn on 5 December, 1835, driving the Mexicans out of the town – where Milam was killed by a sniper – and into the Alamo, where a week later they surrendered.

The Mission San Antonio de Valero – to give the Alamo its full name – had been established in 1718. It is said its name came from the fact that during the Revolutionary War it was used as a barrack by Mexican troops from Alamo de Parras. The four-acre mission included adobe barracks, a convent, and the chapel, surrounded by the quadrangle walls. Abandoned in 1793, the chapel had fallen into disrepair, but although the roof had fallen in, the walls were still firm and stout, and the convent buildings in fair repair.

This became the headquarters of the Texians, or at least of those who remained in San Antonio – on 20 December, some two hundred of their fellows decided to follow commander Colonel Frank Johnson on a freebooting expedition into Mexico, taking most of the existing supplies, clothing and money with them. Johnston handed the command to Colonel James C. Neill who, knowing he did not have enough men to hold his position against the Mexican army that was being formed, wrote to the Governor asking for reinforcements, or for permission to retreat.

Knowing that San Antonio would be Santa Anna's first objective, Governor Henry Smith concluded that if Santa Anna could be forced to leave it in Texian hands, such a defeat might well destroy his power and the confidence of his army. And there was another factor: the Texian army was still anything but strong. General Samuel Houston needed time to recruit enough men to face Santa Anna and defeat him. So the Alamo must not be abandoned.

Instead, in January, 1836, the young, ambitious Colonel William Barret Travis was ordered to take command of the Alamo. Travis balked: he was, he wrote to the Governor 'unwilling to risk my reputation (which is ever dear to a soldier), by going into the enemy's country with such little means, with so few men, and them so badly equipped.'

Nevertheless, he went, taking thirty recruits with him. Tall, red-headed, Travis was at this time nearly thirty-four years of age, and already had a reputation as a firebrand and a fighter. When he arrived at the Alamo, he found himself in the difficult position of having to share his responsibilities because Colonel James Bowie, who had taken command, was senior in age and service.

Soldier of fortune Jim Bowie, born in Kentucky in 1795, had come to Texas in search of the lost San Saba Mine, and in 1828 married Ursula, the daughter of Juan Martin de Veramendi. In 1833, however, his wife and children died in a cholera epidemic and he left Texas, returning a year later to join the Texians in their fight for independence, even though he was a staunch friend of the Mexicans. Somewhere along the line, Bowie had made or acquired the knife which, if not his own exploits, made the name legendary.

On 23 February, the advance guard Santa Anna's five-thousand-strong army reached San Antonio de Bexar and drove the Texians from the town to the shelter of the mission. Shortly after this, David Crockett arrived at the Alamo with nineteen men, the 'Tennessee Mounted Volunteers'. Crockett's name was already legendary. Born in Greene County, Tennessee, in 1786, his colourful career had already included marriage to Polly Finley (a descendant of Macbeth, King of Scotland), election to the Territorial Legislature in 1821, and later to Congress. He was close to fifty years of age at this time.

On 23 February, the Mexican army positioned itself around the walls of the mission, and Santa Anna demanded the surrender of the garrison. Travis answered this demand with a cannon shot, and the hoisting of the new flag, a white, red and green banner with two stars (one for Texas, the other for Coahuila) instead of the Mexican eagle and serpent. Santa Anna replied by hoisting a blood-red flag with a black skull and crossbones, signal of 'no quarter' – no surrender to be accepted, no mercy given – and commenced bombarding the beleaguered mission before retiring to formulate his plans for attack on the Alamo.

Next day, Travis wrote his undying words:

TO THE PEOPLE OF TEXAS AND ALL AMERICANS IN THE WORLD:

Fellow citizens and compatriots – I am besieged by a thousand or more Mexicans under Santa Anna – I have sustained a continual bombardment and cannonade for twenty-four hours and have not lost a man – the enemy has demanded surrender at discretion, otherwise the garrison is to be put to the sword if the fort is taken – I have answered the demands with a cannon shot, and our flag still waves proudly from the walls – I shall never surrender or retreat. Then, I call upon you in the name of liberty, of patriotism and everything dear to the American character, to come to our aid with all dispatch – the enemy is receiving reinforcements daily, and will no doubt increase to three or four thousand in four or five days. If this call is neglected, I am determined to sustain myself as long as possible, and die like a soldier who never forgets what is due his own honour and that of his country – victory or death.

William Barret Travis

Travis then sent his old school friend James Butler Bonham to enlist the aid of Colonel James W. Fannin, stationed at Goliad. Fannin started out at once, but after a series of accidents and unable to get his artillery across the rain-swollen rivers, he reluctantly turned back. When Bonham got ready to return to the Alamo, Fannin tried to stop him.

'I will report to Travis or die in the attempt,' Bonham told him, and set out immediately.

Bonham got back on the afternoon of 3 March and his news was passed to the men – reinforcements were on the way (in fact, they never arrived). In the Mexican camp there was also good news: the arrival of three more battalions, reinforcing Santa Anna's army by nearly a thousand men. Tradition – and it may be no more than that – has it that at this point, Travis drew a line in the sand with his sword, and invited all those who would stay with him to fight the enemy to step across to his side. Every man bar one stepped across, Jim Bowie in his cot asking to be lifted over. (The one dissenter, it is said (and this, too, may be legend) was Louis Moses Rose, an old French teamster from Nacogdoches who had brought in a pack train some weeks before and who returned to his home town some weeks after the siege of the Alamo).

Travis then wrote to a friend in Washington County asking him to take care of his son:

> *'If the country should be saved I may make him a splendid fortune, but if the country should be lost and I should perish, he would have nothing but the proud recollection that he is the son of a man who died for his country. I shall continue to hold the Alamo until I get relief from my countrymen or I perish in its defence. For liberty and honor, God and Texas, victory or death!'*

He also wrote to the newly-assembled Convention at Washington-on-the-Brazos to tell them he felt confident:

> *... that the determined valor and desperate courage heretofore shown by my men will not fail them in the last struggle; and although they may be sacrificed to the vengeance of a Gothic enemy, the victory will cost him so dear, that it will be worse for him than a defeat. For liberty and honor, God and Texas, victory or death!*

Melodramatic? Perhaps – but remember those words were written as shells burst against the old walls of the Alamo, and rain poured down on the huddled men watching the glowing lights of a thousand camp-fires.

By 4 March, the eleventh day of the siege, the garrison was surrounded, its water supply cut off. Cannonballs battered the mission, and riflemen in their pits kept up an incessant fusillade upon the defenders as Santa Anna and his generals determined their final assault. When General Almonte, Santa Anna's aide, remarked that he feared the attack would cost them dear, Santa Anna snapped it was of 'no importance what the cost was, it must be done.'

On 6 March at dawn, the band struck up the assassin's song, the 'Deguello,' confirmation of Santa Anna's instruction that no quarter was to be given. The rocket battery fired to signal the start of the assault and the quiet Sunday morning was shattered by shouts and orders as the Texians rushed to their posts on the walls and the Mexican troops under General Castrillon moved towards them. The Toluca Battalion, heading the attack, fell back hastily as the deadly fire of the Texian riflemen decimated their ranks. General Cos came up, and split half his force into four columns. He was to make simultaneous attacks on the east and west sides, whilst the main attack would come from forces massed on the plain to the north.

Realizing that the east and west attacks were feints, the defenders rushed to the north wall to repel the main attack, whereupon Santa Anna threw reinforcements against the east wall, and it was there that cannon fire made the first breach. Bonham and Travis, both manning artillery, were killed in this attack, the latter by a shot through the forehead. Now Santa Anna ordered the assault on the north walls renewed and as the Mexican troops poured in, the battle became a series of isolated hand-to-hand encounters. Some sixty Texians escaped the Alamo, and heading east on the Gonzales road they were cut down mercilessly by the Mexican cavalry. Jim Bowie was bayonetted to death on his sickbed, fighting to the last. Robert Evans, detailed to blow up the powder magazine, was killed on the threshold of the chapel as he ran towards it. Davy Crockett and a band of men had retreated slowly towards the chapel and Crockett fell near it, surrounded by dead Mexicans. Recently, it has been claimed that Crockett did not die fighting, but that he was one of five (or seven) men who offered to surrender on condition that their lives be spared, but Santa Anna spurned them, and they were cut to pieces with cavalry sabres. Historians still argue over whether it ever happened.

When the ceasefire bugles finally sounded an hour and a half after the battle had begun, the place was like a charnel-house, the dead littered everywhere and the wounded screaming for help. At the time Mexican losses were variously estimated between one and three thousand men, although it is more likely that the total was in the region of perhaps sixty or seventy killed and perhaps three hundred wounded. Santa Anna refused to bury the American dead and gave orders that they be put into a pile and burned.

Don José Francisco Ruiz, alcalde [Mayor] of San Antonio, later wrote:

> *...about three o'clock in the afternoon we laid wood and dry branches upon which the pile of dead bodies was placed, more wood was piled on them, and another pile of bodies was brought and in this manner they were all arranged in layers. Kindling wood was distributed throughout the pile and about five o'clock...it was lighted.*

The funeral pyre was still burning as the Mexicans moved out from the Alamo, taking with them the wife of the gunnery officer, Susanna Dickinson, her daughter Angelina, and Travis's black servant Joe, the only Americans to survive the carnage (although some ten or more Mexicans also came out alive). Eventually under a light breeze the ashes of the 183 brave men who died there – not just Americans, but English, Scottish, Irish, German and Danish as well – were blown gently across the yard, now hallowed ground to the people of Texas and of America.

By holding Santa Anna's army at bay and inflicting such grave casualties, the men who died at the Alamo, who never even knew that Texas had declared its independence from Mexico while the battle was still raging, gave the wavering Texians both a breathing space and a cause. Sam Houston, that bold, shrewd man, hit exactly the right note when he addressed his army just forty-six days later on the eve of the battle of San Jacinto. 'Victory is certain!' he told them. 'Trust in God and fear not! And remember the Alamo! Remember the Alamo!'

Next day the Texians routed Santa Anna's army and shattered the hold of Mexico upon their land once and for all. Today's Texians still 'remember the Alamo' and the men who died there. And they will tell you proudly that those men were not defeated at all: they were only killed.

By the 1840s, emigration to the West had become a fact of life, people from every state on the map, moving in ever-increasing numbers across the plains, pushing the 'frontier' out to Texas and across what is now Kansas and Nebraska. In 1843 the first wagon trains left for Oregon, 'jumping off' at Westport or Independence. Within a few years the Mormons would gather for the long trek west that would terminate in what is now Utah, then deep in Mexican country. In a vivid word-picture, historian Francis Parkman described travelling upriver to Independence. In St Louis, the hotels were crowded, and 'the gunsmiths and saddlers were kept constantly at work in providing arms and equipment for the different parties of travellers'. On that April day in 1846 the steamboat *Radnor* 'was loaded until the water broke alternately over the guards. Her upper deck was covered with large wagons of a peculiar form, for the Santa Fe trade, and her hold was crammed with goods for the same destination. There were also equipments and provisions of a party of Oregon emigrants, a band of mules and horses, piles of saddles and harness.'

In the boat's cabin were, he wrote, 'Santa Fe traders, gamblers, speculators and adventurers of various descriptions,' while the steerage area at the stern – where travellers who bought the cheapest tickets were crammed in – 'was crowded with Oregon emigrants, "mountain men", negroes and a party of Kansas Indians, who had been on a visit to St Louis.' In Westport and Independence the wagon trains kept saddlers and cobblers, blacksmiths and gun-makers, outfitters and map sellers busy; an outfitter in the small town of Liberty, Missouri declared he needed two thousand pounds of bacon a week to keep up with demand.

From the river the wagon trains moved out across the flat, baking, featureless plains, making maybe fifteen miles a day. Their route took them along the Kansas River (to where Fort Kearney would be built in 1848 to protect the trail), then along the Platte to Fort Laramie and on to the headwaters of the Sweetwater River. Over South Pass in the Wind River Mountains they rumbled, and on to Fort Bridger, established in 1842, then along the trail pioneered by Wyeth and the mountain men to Fort Hall, along the Snake River to Fort Boise, and overland to Fort Walla Walla at the confluence of the Snake and the Columbia. Finally, they would follow the Columbia in the footsteps of Lewis and Clark to Fort William, where Portland stands today.

Emigrants to California followed the same route as far as Fort Hall, then turned southeast, bypassing the Great Salt Lake that Jim Bridger had once thought was the Pacific Ocean. They then followed the Humboldt River across what would later become Nevada, then up through the Sierra Nevada and down the western slope to John Sutter's fort near Sacramento and, later, to San Francisco.

Whichever route the emigrants took their journey was slow – the eight-hundred mile (1280km) overland journey could take any-where from two to five months – and was fraught with danger. Every night the wagons would be formed into a square or circle, to keep the animals inside and marauding Indians out. Hostile Indians were not a problem until the mid-1850s, but in 1854 an incident near Fort Laramie involving the shooting by an Indian of a cow which belonged to some Mormon emigrants led to a fight in which Sioux warriors killed Lieutenant John Grattan and his entire command of twenty-nine men and an interpreter.

Indians were not the only problem: rivers could flood, wagons break down, draft animals die. Asiatic cholera, dysentery, snakebite, an accidentally broken bone, sunstroke on the baking plains or frostbite in the freezing mountain passes could spell disaster and even death – and often did. It was said that by 1850 there were four graves to the mile between St Joseph, Missouri and Fort Laramie; eight years later, 'the traveller could find his way (to Oregon) with no other compass than his nose alone' – following the stench of animals that had died and been left to rot along the trail.

In the beginning these primitive trans-continental highways were not so much marked as 'known' by the guides and scouts – many of them one-time mountain men – that the emigrants hired to take them across country. But as in every other human endeavour, there were charlatans, and none bigger than Lansford W. Hastings, an author-adventurer who had accompanied a wagon train to Oregon in 1842, then moved to California.

In 1845, he touted a new, shorter route to California in his book *The Emigrants' Guide to Oregon and California* and set himself up as a guide at Fort Bridger to take emigrants along a route he modestly called the 'Hastings cut-off' which would reduce their journey time to 120 days. In 1846, this totally unreliable 'guide' led a wagon train organized in Springfield, Illinois into what became one of the most tragic episodes in the history of the American West.

THE DONNER PARTY

Of all the California-bound emigrants who braved the myriad hardships of the westward trek, none suffered worse than the Donner Party, a group of eighty-seven men, women and children, organized and led by two wealthy brothers, Jacob and George Donner, who pointed their wagons westward in the summer of 1846.

On 11 May of that year, George Donner's wife Tamsen sent her sister a letter of farewell from the bustling town of Independence. 'I can give you no idea of the hurry of the place at this time,' she wrote. 'It is supposed there will be 7000 waggons start from this place... We go to California, to the bay of Francisco. It is a four month trip. We have three waggons furnished with food and clothing and drawn by three yoke of oxen each... I am willing to go and have no doubt it will be an advantage to our children and to us.'

Although Tamsen Donner was misinformed about the number of wagons leaving Independence that year (the figure was nearer 700 than 7000), her excitement and anticipation are clear. On 12 May the Donner party set out on their journey. The route they would follow was shaped – very roughly speaking – like a rainbow, one end in Missouri, the other California, with the top of the arc at the 8000ft high (2439m) South Pass in Wyoming. On its western side the trail divided, the right fork leading on to Oregon, the left to California.

The Donners had read Hastings' book, and contacted him to conduct them from Fort Bridger, 'thence bearing west southwest, to the Salt Lake; and thence continuing down to the Bay of St Francisco.' When they reached the Fort on 3 August, 1846, however, they learned that Hastings had already gone, leading another wagon train, but he had left word that he would mark the trail for them. They set out at once, following Hastings' trail. At the Red Fork crossing of Weber River, they found a note left by Hastings jammed into a forked stick, telling them the route ahead was very bad and asking them to wait; he would return shortly to show them a better and shorter route he had discovered through the Wasatch Mountains. They would soon discover that this, like all Hastings' promises, was an empty one.

Eight days later he had still not appeared, so the Donners decided to send three men, Charlie Stanton, Bill McCutchen and James Reed, one of the leaders of the party, to find him. They caught up with Hastings but he flatly refused to leave the train he was with; instead he took James Reed to the summit of Big Mountain and showed him – by pointing – the best way to get through the mountains. Stanton and McCutchen remained with the Hastings party to rest their horses and Reed returned to the wagon train alone. A conference was called and it was decided to try the route Hastings had recommended.

The route – there was no trail – proved to be virtually impassable, clogged with willow and alder and strewn with huge boulders. After heartbreaking hardships, the Donner party finally found their way through the Wasatch range and reached the valley south of the Great Salt Lake, having taken what would be eighteen critical days to get there.

It took them another six days and nights to cross the empty salt desert – a journey Hastings''guide' had told them would take two. To speed their progress, the emigrants decided that most of the furniture and other valuables they had brought from Illinois would have to be abandoned, along with four wagons and most of the livestock which had stampeded for water when they were unyoked. The days were murderously hot, the nights freezing. And still no word from Hastings.

McCutchen and Stanton, now back with the train, were sent ahead to get help and food from Sutter's Fort, while the rest of the party – now down to fifteen wagons from the original twenty-three – struggled onward to the base of the Sierra as geese on their way south honked ominously overhead.

By now the emigrants were exhausted, both physically and emotionally, riven by quarrels and petty spites. In the course of trying to prevent an argument between two of the men, John Reed stabbed one of them to death: as a result he was banished from the desert, leaving his wife and five children with the wagon train. He determined to try to get to California alone and bring help.

On 19 October, 'Little Charlie' Stanton returned from Sutter's Fort with two Indian guides and five mules laden with much-needed supplies, giving the party new hope. On 23 October, the pioneers left the salt desert behind and reached water. Ahead of them lay the long climb over the mountains. The wagons were strung out in several groups now, everyone anxious to get through the pass before snow closed it. It was now 3 November and snow had already fallen.

Part of the group – twenty-one souls, twelve of them children – stopped in Alder Creek valley; the larger group in the lead camped near a lake (now called Donner Lake) high in the mountains, ready for the final push through the pass and into the valley. That night, however, a month earlier than usual, the first storm of the winter struck, and it was a bad one.

They fashioned shelters of wagon canvas and huddled together to keep out the winter cold. It snowed for eight days, blocking the pass. Marooned a mile high in the Sierra Nevada, all they could do now was wait – and hope. By 4 December the snow was eight feet deep. By the middle of the month, their situation was desperate, and it was decided someone must go for help, or they would all die from hunger.

Seventeen of the strongest survivors (ten men, five women, and two boys) who called themselves the 'Forlorn Hope,' set out on home-made snowshoes to try to reach Sutter's Fort, over a hundred miles distant. Led by Will Eddy they left on 16 December with six days' rations on what became a nightmare of privation and horror that lasted thirty-two days.

On Christmas night they were caught in a violent storm. Totally lost, utterly exhausted, they had no food and no hope in such weather of finding any; two days later four of them were dead. The survivors cut flesh from the bodies and cooked it, weeping as they ate. The remaining flesh was labelled so that no one would eat his kindred, and the band moved on. Two more men died, and eventually even the two Indians, who had steadfastly refused to touch human flesh, were shot and eaten. Finally, on 10 January, 1847, in chilling rain the seven survivors happened upon an Indian village. A week later Will Eddy reached a settlement called Johnson's Ranch and help was sent for.

Heavy storms blanketed the Sierra throughout January, so it was not until February that a seven-man relief party from Sutters Fort led by Aquilla Glover reached the survivors – if these walking skeletons could be called that. It was clear many were far too weak and ill to be brought out, so Glover and his men brought down only those who were strong enough to travel: three men, four women, and seventeen children. On the way down they met McCutchen and John Reed who were going up to the camps, bringing desperately needed food and clothing.

The Glover party reached Fort Sutter on 4 March. In the meantime Reed and McCutchen had got through to the lake camp where they found evidence that the starving emigrants had also been reduced to cannibalism, as had those at the Alder Creek camp. Jacob Donner was dead, his brother George was dying. Although Reed begged her to come with him, Tamsen Donner would not leave her husband. The two men headed back down the mountain with fourteen children and three adults.

A fourth relief party led by William Fallon set out to bring down the remaining survivors on 13 April. When they reached the lake camp they were truly appalled by what they found – human remains in cooking pots, body parts scattered everywhere. Many had died, others had been killed for their flesh. They found only one person alive, a man named Keseberg who the rescuers suspected had murdered – and eaten – Tamsen Donner.

Fallon's party reached Sutter's Fort on 26 April. Of the eighty-nine emigrants who had set out so optimistically from Fort Bridger only forty-seven came through alive.

It is difficult to imagine any tragedy worse than this, but there would be many more like it as the West opened up, and it must have seemed during those early years that it was opening up at an extraordinary pace. In 1845, the United States acquired further huge areas of land when the Republic of Texas, which had thrown off the shackles of Mexican domination by defeating the Mexican army at San Jacinto six weeks after the fall of the Alamo, abandoned its original intention of remaining permanently independent and was annexed to become the twenty-eighth American State just five days before James K. Polk took the presidential oath of office. The absorption of Texas, however, virtually guaranteed war with Mexico, which had never accepted the independence of its rebellious province.

So the $100,000,000 war with Mexico was fought and won when its capital was captured. This too was Manifest Destiny: under the terms of Mexico's surrender – the Treaty of Guadalupe Hidalgo – the victorious United States appropriated the northern third of the republic, a vast stretch of land which comprised all of western Texas, Nevada, Utah, Arizona and California and parts of New Mexico, Colorado and Wyoming.

The sum paid to Mexico for this huge area – exactly the same amount that Thomas Jefferson had paid for Louisiana Territory – proved to be an even bigger bargain: just nine days before the Treaty was signed, a man named James Marshall discovered gold in the American River at a settlement called Sutter's Mill, near what is now Coloma, California. A few months later when the news reached the

East, the California Gold Rush began and the movement of Americans westward became an irresistible force.

Oglala Sioux chiefs Red Cloud (1822–1909), left, and American Horse (1840–1908) in Deadwood, South Dakota. Perhaps the best-known Indian chief, Red Cloud opposed the US army's proposition to build a fort and roads through his tribal territory in Wyoming, and forced them to abandon their plans.

CHAPTER THREE

FIGHTING INDIANS

A T FIRST, the Native Americans who lived and hunted in the hitherto virgin lands of the trans-Mississippi West took little notice of the gradual invasion of their country. Many of the mountain men who were their first contact with the white man had taken Indian wives, learned something of the native language, and tried to live in peace with the Indians. But as the fur traders increased in number, and as the fur companies made deals with the Indians, setting one tribe against another or against trappers working for rival organizations, hostile encounters between them and the white men became more frequent and more deadly.

Along the Mississippi lived the Chippewa, Santee Sioux, Fox and Sauk. On the northern plains were the warlike Shoshone and the Sioux, or Lakota, split into various subtribes: Oglala, Teton, Yankton. To the south of their lands were the hunting grounds of the Cheyenne and Arapaho and further south again in the deserts and on the southern plains were Arapaho, Comanche, Kiowa and Apache and what were known as 'pueblo' Indians: Navajo, Zuni and Hopi among them. On the Pacific coast were Modocs, Flatheads, Diggers, Nez Percé. Each tribe would – sooner or later – experience the shock of invasion and the submersion of their identity in the irresistible tide of western expansion.

Each tribe reacted in its own way. Each tribe rejected the proposition that the Indian should cease doing what he had always done and be like the white man, on the not unreasonable proposition that if they were to suggest the white man should live like the Indians, he would as readily refuse. But what few, if any of them, knew was that from the time of Christopher Columbus' first landing in the New World three and a half centuries earlier, the white man's dealings with the Indian tribes of the East had been conducted only one way: treacherously and ruthlessly.

The first English-speaking settlers who arrived in Virginia in 1607 set a golden crown on the head of Wahunsonacook, leader of the Powhatan tribe, and then shamelessly put his people to work providing food for the newcomers. When one of them, John Rolfe, married his daughter Pocahontas, Wahunsonacook became more English than Indian, losing contact with his own people. After the old chief died, the vengeful Powhatans rose against the interlopers, but they reckoned without the firepower of English guns. Soon where there had been some eight thousand Powhatans there were less than a thousand. Of those remaining thousand, now only Pocahontas is remembered.

In Massachusetts it was the same. In 1675, in what was called King Philip's War (like the Virginian colonists, the settlers there had crowned a chief named Metacom and renamed him) the Wampanoag and the Narragansett Indians rose up against the white men, destroying twelve of their villages, but after months of fighting were themselves almost exterminated. Again and again, one after another, the great tribes were sucked into conflict and then annihilated – the Iroquois, the Miamis of the Ohio Valley, the Ottawas led by Pontiac, the Shawnees under Tecumseh. Driven from their native lands, scattered to the wind, the eastern woodland tribes dwindled and died out one after another, only their musical names remaining:

Pequot and Montauk, Chickahominy and Huron, Chesapeake, Seneca, Mohawk, Erie and Mohican.

In 1832 Ma-ka-tai-me-she-kia-kiak, called Black Hawk, a leader of the Sauk Indians who had fought alongside the British in the War of 1812, refused to be deported to Iowa and formed an alliance with the Winnebagos, the Pottawotamies and the Kickapoos and made war on the new white settlements in northern Illinois. It was estimated that some seventy whites and between four hundred and six hundred Indians died in Black Hawk's War before he was betrayed and captured. He was taken East, imprisoned and then put on display. After he died, the governor of Iowa Territory obtained his skeleton and kept it in his office as a souvenir.

In 1830 the US government implemented President Andrew Jackson's recommendation that the Cherokee, Chickasaw, Choctaw, Creek and Seminole Indians still clinging stubbornly to their tribal lands should be relocated in 'an ample district west of the Mississippi ... to be guaranteed to the Indians as long as they shall occupy it.' A Commissioner of Indian Affairs was appointed to ensure that new laws affecting the Indians were properly carried out, but before they could be put into effect, emigrants had already flooded westward into the territories of Iowa and Minnesota, requiring a shifting of the 'permanent Indian frontier' from the Mississippi River to the 95th meridian (which runs north-south through Minnesota and Iowa, skirting Kansas City, Missouri and Dallas, Texas, to Galveston on the Gulf of Mexico).

When in 1838 the Cherokees were dispossessed, rounded up – with the usual callous brutality – and marched in the bitter depths of winter from Georgia across Tennessee, Alabama, Kentucky, and then Arkansas to the south-eastern quadrant of the new 'Indian Territory', one in four of the estimated seventeen thousand men, women and children who had begun the trek died from cold, hunger or disease. The survivors remembered the removal as ' The Trail of Tears.' Americans remembered it in a jaunty song:

> *All I want in this creation*
> *Is a pretty little girl and a big plantation*
> *Way down yonder in the Cherokee nation.*

When, just ten short years later, word reached the East of the discovery of gold in California, and hundreds of thousands of eager Easterners headed for the goldfields to get rich, no one any longer cared about treaties that had promised the frontier lands to the Indians 'for as long as the grass shall grow'. The Indians were a hindrance, incapable of assimilation, obsolete. In 1850, California became the thirty-first state, although needless to say, none of the Pacific coast Indians were consulted. When gold was discovered in Colorado in 1858, further hordes of prospectors and settlers swarmed across the plains, their wagons decorated with the slogan 'Pike's Peak or bust!' Denver became a boom town, Kansas and Nebraska territories were organized, and that same year Minnesota became a state. These developments appropriated nearly all the hunting grounds of the Plains tribes

This, the white man said again, was America's Manifest Destiny: to command and to own the land, the rivers, the forests, the mountains and all that was in them. However, the white man would find that fulfilling that destiny would take considerably longer than he anticipated, for awaiting him was implacable opposition. On the northern Plains it would be the Sioux and their allies the Cheyenne, on the southern the Comanche. In the deserts of the Southwest were the Apache. They wanted nothing to do with the settlements that were appearing on the lands to the east, the stagecoaches plying across them, the forts being built by the pony soldiers. Let the white man come, they said, and we will fight him.

FIGHTING INDIANS

The white man, however, was otherwise engaged, fighting a war with himself, a war between the states, the US Civil War. As a result, the forts and military posts of the West were drained of experienced soldiers, and the raw young volunteers who replaced them were far from being the equals of the native warriors of the plains. And soon, the first real Indian war broke out.

LITTLE CROW'S WAR

Short and bloody though it was, Little Crow's War came where it was least expected, in a remote corner of southern Minnesota not far from an insignificant army post called Fort Ridgely. There, the once-proud woodland Sioux known as the Santee had surrendered their tribal lands and were crammed into a narrow reservation – still there today – along the Minnesota River, where crooked agents and greedy traders systematically cheated them out of the food and annuities promised to them by the government in exchange for their land.

In the summer of 1862, when the Santees gathered to exchange these annuities, they were told the money had not arrived and therefore no food could be distributed. When they angrily protested, the agent called for soldiers to guard the store and the food in it. On 4 August, five hundred Santee men surrounded the soldiers while others broke into the store and helped themselves to food. Further trouble was averted when the commanding officer wisely turned a blind eye, later persuading the Indian Agent, Thomas Galbraith, to issue meat and flour 'on credit,' as it were.

Ta-oya-te-duta, or Little Crow, leader of the Santee Sioux, had taken the 'white man's road', become a Christian, done his best to change with the times. When, on 15 August, Galbraith broke his promise to issue more food because the money had still not arrived, Little Crow spoke up in bitter anger on behalf of his people:

We have waited a long time. The money is ours but we cannot get it. We have no food, but here are these stores filled with food. We ask that you, the agent, make some arrangement by which we can get food from the stores, or else we may take our own way to keep ourselves from starving. When men are hungry they help themselves.

Galbraith turned to the nearby traders and asked them what he should do. One of them, Andrew Myrick, replied contemptuously 'So far as I am concerned if they are hungry let them eat grass or their own shit.' Mortally insulted, Little Crow and his men stalked away. Were the white men so stupid they did not know the hot-headed young men of the tribe were talking of making war?

Two days later, on 17 August, 1860 a group of young Santees were on their way back from an unsuccessful hunting trip; to appease his hunger one of them stole some eggs. Another warned him he would get into trouble for stealing from a white farmer. This grew into an argument in which some of the young men began taunting the others, calling them cowards who were afraid of the white man. The upshot of this childish squabble was that to prove their lack of fear the four men burst into a house where several white families had gathered for Sunday services and in an act of bravado at once barbaric, deadly and dreadful, hacked three men and two women to bits.

Late that night a council of the headmen of the tribe was called. Although some of those present were for peace, the majority reasoned that the tribe would be punished whatever they did, and that it would be better to make a pre-emptive strike against the white men. Little Crow, his face haggard, great beads of sweat on his forehead, was not so sure. 'The white men are like locusts,' he said. 'They fly so thick the whole sky is like a snowstorm. We are only little herds of buffalo left scattered.'

'Little Crow is a coward!' one of the younger men shouted. Angered by this insult Little Crow made an impassioned speech to those present. Little Crow was not a coward, he said. But he knew what would happen. 'Kill one, two, ten,' he warned, 'and ten times ten will come to kill you. Count your fingers all day long and white men with guns in their hands will come faster than you can count... Braves, you are little children – you are fools. You will die like rabbits when the hungry wolves hunt them in the hard moon of January.' Nevertheless, he agreed to lead the raid, sending messengers to summon the other sub-tribes down the valley. Tomorrow they would attack the Agency.

Next day at dawn the war party attacked white families living near the Agency, killing twenty-three men and abducting ten women and children, emptying the warehouse of provisions and then setting fire to it. After they left, post-trader Andrew Myrick was found dead, his mouth stuffed full of grass.

Other war parties attacked and burned houses in a thirty mile radius, killing and scalping males and children, raping the women, stealing animals. It was estimated that the death toll on the first day of the rising was high in the hundreds.

When fugitives who had managed to get across the Minnesota River reached Fort Ridgely, thirteen miles downriver, Captain John Marsh, commanding, rushed a detachment of forty-seven men down to the ferry crossing, where they were ambushed by the waiting Santees. Attempting to lead his men across the river, Marsh was swept away and drowned; more than half of his demoralized troopers were slain trying to fight their way back to the Fort.

Fighting continued on the second day, and on the third, 19 August, Little Crow led his warriors to the Fort and laid siege to it. For three days the Indians tried unsuccessfully to breach the defences, but every time they charged they were repelled by the massed rifles of the defenders and double charges of canister shot, losing many lives.

At sundown on 22 August the Sioux pulled away and instead decided to attack the nearby New Ulm, a town of perhaps nine hundred inhabitants, but already crowded with refugees. Alerted by earlier raids by Santee warriors on 19 August, the townspeople had built barricades, brought in more weapons, and been reinforced by militiamen from towns further down the valley. Fighting a desperate rearguard action from house to house the New Ulmers held off the Santees until their leader Mankato – Little Wolf – (Little Crow had been wounded and did not take part) broke off the fight and retreated, leaving something like two hundred buildings burning or in ruins and more than a hundred casualties among the citizenry.

By now word of the uprising had reached St Paul, and a force of 1400 militiamen of the 6th Minnesota Regiment marched to the rescue under the command of General Henry Hastings Sibley (1811–1891) a former fur trader and Governor of Minnesota. Sibley's force reached Fort Ridgely three days after the battle of New Ulm. The Santees retreated up the Minnesota valley, taking with them a hundred or so prisoners, most of them women and children. Meanwhile, marauding bands of warriors raided white settlements at random, burning, looting and killing.

After a number of hard fought battles and even an exchange of letters discussing an armistice, the two forces met for the last time on 23 September at Wood Lake in 'a long and well-contested battle', where an elaborate ambush laid by the Santee leader went wrong, leaving many of Little Wolf's men unable to participate in the fight. Outnumbered two to one by Sibley's soldiers, the Santee were cut to pieces. They retreated in disorder, leaving the body of Mankato on the field. Three days later Sibley captured the main Santee camp and freed 150 female captives, most if not all of whom had been raped and otherwise mistreated.

Knowing reprisals would follow, the Santee scattered in an effort to save themselves, but Sibley was relentless. Scouring the countryside he arrested every Indian he encountered until he had some two thousand prisoners in custody, the majority of them peaceful Sioux who had taken no part in the uprising. Within a month some four hundred of the likeliest offenders had been 'tried' – each hearing averaging about ten minutes – and over three hundred of them sentenced to death by hanging for the crimes of murder, rape, or engaging in battle. Appalled by the thought of mass executions on this scale, an Episcopal bishop named Henry Whipple appealed to President Abraham Lincoln for clemency; Lincoln ruled Indians could not be hanged for going to war. Only those who had committed rape and murder would be hanged.

Meanwhile Sibley was still holding the remaining 1,700 Santees – mostly women and children – prisoner, although the only crime they were accused of was being Indian. He ordered them to be marched to Fort Snelling, about a hundred miles distant. On the way they were stoned and clubbed by angry citizens; one child was snatched from its mother's arms and beaten to death. Meanwhile, the condemned prisoners, taken first to a prison camp, and later to a stockade near the town of Mankato, were also attacked by would-be lynch mobs.

On 6 December President Lincoln instructed Sibley that he should 'cause to be executed' thirty-nine of the convicted men, holding the others subject to further orders. The execution date was set for the day after Christmas. Shortly after 10 a.m. on that bitterly cold morning thirty-eight prisoners (one man had been reprieved) were marched from the prison to the scaffold, singing their death songs as they walked. They kept singing as the soldiers put white hoods over their heads and looped the nooses around their necks until, on a signal from the officer, the control rope was cut and the sound abruptly ceased.

The day of the Santee was over. Most of their war chiefs and warriors were dead; the few who were left, imprisoned or in exile. Their lands were confiscated, and the survivors were banished to a reservation at Crow Creek in Dakota Territory. The first shipment of 770 left St Paul by boat on 3 May, 1863, showered by stones from citizens lining the banks of the river.

Little Crow, who had fled to Canada with some of his people, unwisely decided in June of the following year to return to Minnesota to steal horses; he seems not to have known that the state had instituted a bounty for Sioux scalps. On the afternoon of 3 July 1864, farmer Nat Lampon and his son Chauncey, out hunting, spotted Little Crow and his son picking raspberries and (although he had no idea who they were) opened fire, killing Little Wolf. The state presented the hunters who had killed him with the promised bounty of $25 plus a bonus of five hundred dollars. The old chief's son learned later that his father's scalp and skull had been placed on display in St Paul.

Little Crow's 'war' was in many ways a template of all the 'wars' between the Native American tribes and the white man that followed: there would not be a single State or Territory west of the Mississippi that did not experience one. The only difference between them was one of scale. Everywhere the sheer volume of white expansion forced the two sides into more and more contact, with increasingly violent reactions on the part of the Indians as they resisted the advance.

That such resistance was doomed from the start, the Indians could not know; but it was. Not only were the Indians comprehensively outnumbered and catastrophically outgunned but also because of the very nature of their concept of warfare. In almost every tribe there existed a cult of bravery, one that considered individual acts of courage or cunning far more admirable than mere killing. Their inter-tribal wars were a state of permanent hostility punctuated by raids to capture booty and to exhibit courage; because symbolic death –'counting coup' by touching an enemy with a stick and escaping unharmed – was valued far more than killing an enemy, deaths in battle were comparatively few. It was a concept the white man never could and never would understand. Their outlook was brutally pragmatic: dead men don't shoot back.

So in Colorado, when white settlers became convinced the local Arapaho and Cheyenne were only waiting for their opportunity to attack them, as Little Crow had attacked the settlements of Minnesota, white leaders reacted quickly. Prominent among these was a former Methodist minister named John Milton Chivington (1821-1894). A hero of the war against the Confederates in New Mexico who had been named commander of the Military District of Colorado, Chivington was, it was said, keen to run for Congress and anxious to earn promotion to the rank of brigadier general.

MASSACRE AT SAND CREEK

On 28 September, 1864, Chivington sat in on a council at Denver between Governor John Evans and Indian peace leaders Black Kettle and White Antelope of the Cheyenne, and Left Hand of the Arapahos. Expressing their desire for peace and safety, the Indians were instructed to submit to the authorities at Fort Lyon, and await instructions for formal surrender. They handed over half of their weapons to the military and made camp on Sand Creek, 40 miles north of the fort; it was estimated approximately five hundred men women and children in about one hundred lodges were present.

But public feeling in Denver was running high against the

Indians – any Indians. Wagon trains had been scourged, helpless settlers killed. Nobody – least of all a blustering religious fanatic looking for glory and promotion like Colonel John Chivington – cared whether it had been done by the Comanche, the Sioux, the Kiowa or Cheyenne: the only good Indian was a dead Indian. Heading a six-hundred-man force of rag-tag 'volunteers' he made a forced march upon Fort Lyon. When he expressed his intention of making a dawn attack on the unsuspecting Cheyenne encampment, of 'collecting scalps' and 'wading in gore,' some of his officers protested that such an act would be 'murder in every sense of the word.' Chivington reacted violently. 'Damn any man who sympathizes with Indians!' he raged. 'I have come to kill Indians and believe it is right and honorable to use any means under God's heaven to kill Indians!'

And next day, at eight o'clock in the morning of 28 November he led his troops at the gallop into the unsuspecting Cheyenne village with only one intent in mind: to kill as many Indians as could be killed. Seeing the soldiers coming, Black Kettle ran an American flag up over his tipi – he had been told that as long as the US flag flew above him no soldier would fire upon his people – but that did not prevent the butchery that followed. White Antelope, seventy-five years old, ran out unarmed to confront the advancing troops, shouting 'Stop, stop!' He was cut down mercilessly. Lodges, mostly occupied by women and children – nearly all the warriors were some miles away, hunting – were torn down and the helpless occupants shot or cut down with sabres as they fled.

An eyewitness later testified to the brutality of the attack:

> *There were some thirty or forty (women) collected in a hole for protection. They sent out a little girl about six years old with a white flag on a stick; she had not proceeded but a*

few steps when she was shot and killed. All the (women) in that hole were afterwards killed, and four or five (men) outside... Every one I saw dead was scalped. I saw one (woman) cut open with, as I thought, an unborn child lying by her side ... I saw the body of White Antelope with the privates cut off, and I heard a soldier say he was going to make a tobacco pouch out of them... I saw one (woman) whose privates had been cut out... I saw a little girl about five years of age who had been hid in the sand; two soldiers discovered her, drew their pistols and shot her, and then pulled her out of the sand by the arm. I saw quite a number of infants-in-arms killed with their mothers.

When the slaughter ended, 105 women and children and twenty-eight men were dead (in his official report, Chivington claimed to have killed between four and five hundred warriors). Among the soldiers there were nine dead and thirty-eight wounded, many of the casualties self-inflicted by what we now call 'friendly fire'. Challenged to justify such a barbaric slaughter, Chivington shrugged off the question. 'Nits breed lice' he said, as if that were all the explanation needed.

The Cheyennes never forgot Sand Creek. Forging an alliance with the Sioux (a rising leader named Sitting Bull was among those who smoked the war pipe), Arapaho and Northern Cheyenne, they turned the South Platte into a war zone, ripping out miles of telegraph wires, raiding stage stations, wagon trains and small military outposts, burning the town of Julesburg and scalping its defenders in retaliation for Chivington's atrocities. Further north, in the hunting grounds of the Sioux, another war flared.

A treaty which conceded safe passage to the white man through their lands had been signed by the Sioux in 1865; but the combative

Oglala leader Makhpiya-luta (Red Cloud) rejected it and his warriors continued their depredations to such an extent that a further 'peace commission' was sent to Fort Laramie the following year to negotiate new terms. Unaware that the council was in session, General Henry B. Carrington unwittingly led a column of troops past it. When Red Cloud learned the column was en route to the Powder River country to build a chain of forts to protect the Bozeman Trail over which thousands of emigrants were ready to travel to the new goldfields of Idaho and Montana, he stalked out of the council, openly announcing that he was taking the war path.

Undeterred by Red Cloud's threats Carrington led his men to Piney Creek, a branch of the Powder River, and there on 15 July, 1856, began construction of Fort Phil Kearny. This was equivalent to a declaration of war, even had one still been necessary, and from that moment on, Fort Phil Kearny would never know a peaceful day. Let a soldier show himself in the open, he would be ambushed. Let a herder get out of sight of his guard, he was a dead man. Anyone leaving the confines of the stockade did so knowing he might never see it again. In the first five months of its existence the Sioux killed 154 persons at or near the fort, wounding twenty more and carrying off around seven hundred head of livestock.

Although the stands of timber from which the logs were obtained were some six or seven miles away, the building of the fort continued, with large parties known as 'wood trains' – sometimes as many as 150 strong – felling timber and dragging it to the fort. Again and again General Carrington cautioned his officers never to pursue the Indians who frequently attacked the wood trains beyond the sightlines of lookouts who could signal the fort for help. One of the officers, Captain William Judd Fetterman of the 27th Infantry, had no patience with such tactics. After a skirmish with a war party which had attacked the wood train he boasted 'Give me eighty men and I'll ride through the whole Sioux nation.' Two weeks later he got his chance.

On Friday, 21 December a wood train of fifty-five men left to bring in what Carrington confidently expected would be the last timber needed to complete the fort. At 11 a.m., frantic signals indicated the train was under attack and 'Boots and Saddles' rang out. Captain James Powell was detailed to lead the eighty-one-man rescue party, but Fetterman insisted on taking charge as the senior Infantry officer. All too aware of Fetterman's recklessness, Carrington counselled him not to pursue the Indians beyond Lodge Trail Ridge because his command would not be visible from the fort.

It was shortly after noon by the time Fetterman occupied the ridge with his men in skirmish order. As he did so, the lookout signalled that the wood train was no longer under attack. Not fifty yards or so ahead of him, although of course he did not know who they were, Fetterman saw a handful of warriors which included Big Nose, the brother of the great Cheyenne leader Little Wolf, Hump of the Minneconjous and a young Sioux named Crazy Horse. Their job was to taunt the troops and decoy them into an ambush. Disregarding his orders, Fetterman fell for the ruse and ordered the charge, whereupon the Indians turned tail and ran, the cavalrymen pursuing at full gallop along a narrow ridge and down toward Peno Creek where, concealed in gullies, something like two thousand warriors were waiting for them. Within no more than ten or fifteen blood-spattered minutes of hand-to-hand fighting Fetterman and every single man of his command was dead.

When a relief column reached the scene of the ambush a little while later, the most appalling sight met their eyes. The bodies of the dead had been stripped naked, scalped, mutilated, disembowelled and shot full of arrows. Dead horses were scattered along the trail. When his body was identified, Fetterman was found to have taken his own life. It was the worst defeat the US Army had yet suffered in Indian warfare, and the second in American history from which there were no survivors.

In the spring of 1867 a new face appeared on the Indian frontier. Fresh from his triumphs in the Civil War, a dashing cavalry leader was assigned to lead the newly-formed 7th Cavalry in the campaign against the hostiles. Civil War hero General George Armstrong Custer was already something of a legend, but although he pursued the Indians with much energy, his achievements as part of General Winfield Scott Hancock's ill-organized 1867 campaign were nil. In fact he wound up being court-martialled for being absent without leave, having left his command to ride back halfway across Kansas to visit his wife, Elizabeth Bacon 'Libby' Custer, whom he had married three years earlier.

THE BATTLE OF THE WASHITA

George Armstrong Custer was one of the most picturesque, dashing figures in American military history – and he knew it. Born at New Rumley, Ohio on 5 December, 1839, he was appointed to West Point in 1857 and graduated at the bottom of his class four years later. Assigned as a lieutenant to the 2nd Cavalry, he came to the attention of General McClennan in the Peninsular campaign, serving with distinction through the Gettysburg and Virginia campaigns, and by the age of twenty-six was a major general of volunteers. Typically, it was to Custer that the Confederate flag of truce was borne on 9 April, 1865.

He was a talented writer and author; theatrical and handsome; he wore his blond hair at shoulder length, favoured buckskin coats and wide-brimmed non-regulation hats rather than the dull drab of army blue. He had his own fine horses, his dogs, his faithful retinue of Indian scouts.

He arrived on the frontier at the height of the Cheyenne campaign and one of his first experiences of Indian warfare was finding the brutally mutilated bodies of Lieutenant Kidder, 2nd Cavalry, and his ten men after they were cut off and killed by a band of Sioux while bringing dispatches to Custer from Fort Sedgwick.

Reviewing the failure of the summer campaign – some eight hundred civilians murdered, the Indians again and again escaping from the troops by travelling at night when their trail could not be followed – army commander General Philip Sheridan decided in the autumn of 1868 that his best hope of defeating the Indians was to attack them in their winter camps.

Custer was recalled to active duty, and on 22 November led the 7th Cavalry southward from Camp Supply in the Indian Territory to the Washita River as part of a three-pronged attack: Major Eugene A. Carr with seven troops of the 5th Cavalry heading southeast from Fort Lyon, Colorado, Major Andrew W. Evans with six troops of cavalry and two companies of infantry plus four mountain howitzers, moving eastward from Fort Bascom, New Mexico. Custer's orders from Sheridan were explicit: to locate the hostile tribes, 'to destroy their villages and ponies, to kill or hang all warriors, and bring back all women and children.'

On 26 November, Custer struck the trail of a war party which had been raiding along the Santa Fe Trail and set off in pursuit, continuing the march all night. Reconnoitring in deep snow with an Indian scout, Custer realized he was on top of a large camp and determined to attack it at dawn.

There were two things he did not know. One was that the village was far bigger than he thought, with maybe six thousand Cheyennes, Arapahos, Kiowas and Comanches camped all the way down the river valley. The second was that the tribe camped nearest to where he would attack was that of Black Kettle, just back from an unsuccessful peace parley with General Hazen at Fort Cobb (unsuccessful because, of course, Hazen was fully aware of Sheridan's war plans).

Dividing his command into four units commanded by himself, Major Joel Elliott and Captains Thompson and Myers, Custer surrounded the camp. In the foggy dawn of 27 November bugles sounded the charge and as the 7th Cavalry band struck up the 7th Cavalry's marching song 'Garryowen,' the cavalrymen in their heavy coats and fur hats fell upon the village, the thunder of their horses hoofs muted by the deep snow. In a matter of minutes, Custer's soldiers destroyed the village, and in a like amount of time slaughtered several hundred Indian ponies.

Altogether they killed 103 Cheyennes, although few of them were warriors: among the first to die in the melee were Black Kettle and his wife. Men, women, children ran naked into the frozen river, which soon ran red with their blood; others were trampled under the hooves of charging horses. By 10 o'clock it seemed the fight must be over.

Instead, the gunfire up the valley brought a swarm of Arapaho, Kiowa and Comanche warriors to the scene, where they surrounded a platoon of nineteen soldiers commanded by Major Joel Elliott and wiped them out. By noon Kiowas and Comanches were arriving from downriver and when Custer was told by a captured Indian woman that the camp stretched a further ten miles down the river, he realized the odds were mounting against him. Rounding up the fifty-three women and children he had captured and without even bothering to search for the missing Major Elliott and his men, he set off on a forced march back to Camp Supply. Behind him in the ruined village of Black Kettle were a hundred dead bodies, a mountain of destroyed horses, perhaps seven hundred in all, and the smouldering remnants of more than a thousand buffalo robes, countless saddles, blankets, weapons, clothing, five hundred pounds of lead and an equal amount of powder, and four thousand arrows.

At Camp Supply Sheridan ordered the entire post out for a formal review to welcome Custer home. The band played 'Garryowen' as the victors waved the scalps they had taken and Sheridan congratulated the boy general for 'efficient and gallant services rendered.'

If it was noticed, nothing was said about a potentially fatal flaw in Custer's tactical abilities. At the Washita he ignored a fundamental military precept, attacking an enemy of unknown strength on a battlefield whose terrain was equally unknown. Indeed, when his scout Little Beaver warned him 'Heap Indians down there,' Custer shrugged off the warning with the words 'There are not Indians enough in the country to whip the Seventh Cavalry.' It was an eerie precursor of what was to come.

But at the Washita he was lucky: his force outnumbered the warriors he had to face in Black Kettle's village and the terrain gave him no unexpected problems. Although he was criticized severely for leaving the battlefield without learning what had happened to Captain Joel Elliott and his detachment, the battle of the Washita established Custer in the minds of the American people – and in his own – as master plainsman, renowned hunter, and pre-eminent Indian fighter.

One day in the future, destiny would weave together all of these events: the Sand Creek massacre and the 'battle' of the Washita, Little Crow's war and the 'Battle of the Hundred Slain' (as the Sioux called it) at Fort Phil Kearny, together with the lives of George Armstrong Custer, Sitting Bull and Crazy Horse, all of whom would play pivotal roles in the long, bloody saga of the Indian wars of the West. But not yet; not just yet.

*

On the Great Plains, the white man's most implacable adversary and the greatest barrier to the advance of the frontier was the Sioux, whose territory had at one time stretched from the Great Lakes to the Rockies, from the middle reaches of Canada to the Platte River. They were a proud, noble and accomplished race; General George Crook called them 'the finest light cavalry in the world.' There were others who fought just as bitterly, of course: Cheyennes, Kiowas, Comanches, Nez Percés, Modocs and Pueblos among them.

But in the Southwest the white man met a different and even more deadly opposition – the people called Apache, a word that means the same thing in any native American dialect: 'enemy'. They came, anthropologists believe, across the frozen Bering Staits and filtered slowly south, away from the Arctic cold and the hostile tundra. They called themselves Indeh, 'the People', and in time, imbued with a deadliness and hostility unmatched by any other tribe, they became the masters of the hostile land in which they lived, the desert and mountains of Arizona, New Mexico and northern Chihuaha. From the time of the Conquistadors, their enmity was mainly directed against the citizens of Mexico, but things began to change following the Mexican War and the ceding to the United States of the huge portion of formerly Mexican land known as the Gadsden Purchase. This was and had always been the land of the Apache, but now it became crowded with wagon trains carrying gold hunters to the Californian bonanzas, survey parties and US Army units seeking sites for military posts. Then in the summer of 1851 gold was discovered at Pinos Altos, near present-day Silver City, and a small town soon sprang up on the site.

Although outright warfare between Apache and white man was still some way in the future, raids on small parties became more frequent and more deadly. In April 1854, for example, the Oatman family consisting of father, mother, two sons and four daughters were attacked by a marauding band of Tonto Apaches as they crossed the Gila River. The two adults, two daughters and one son were killed on the spot, the other son left for dead. After looting the wagons the Apaches took the two surviving girls, Olive and Mary Ann, with them, later selling them to some Mojave Indians. Lorenzo, the wounded son, was rescued, and when he recovered from his wounds, began to search for his sisters. He found Olive five years later, almost unrecognizable. The younger girl, Mary Ann, had died of hardships and exposure.

In another raid on an October day in 1860, while its owner was away a band of Apaches attacked a ranch on the Sonoita River that belonged to Irishman Johnny Ward. They plundered the house, running off with a small herd of cattle and kidnapping twelve-year-old Felix, one of the sons of Jesusa Tellez, the Mexican woman who lived with Ward. When the rancher returned, he took his troubles to the US Army at Fort Buchanan, twelve miles away, where the commanding officer, Colonel Pitcairn Morrison, 8th Infantry, fielded a detachment of sixty troopers led by Lieutenant George N. Bascom, 16th Infantry, to search for the missing livestock and child. Bascom knew the warrior leaders of the Apache were Mangas Coloradas (Red Sleeves) of the Mimbres Apaches and Cochise of the Chiricahuas, whose wife was one of Mangas' daughters. And he knew where Cochise was.

SIXTEEN DAYS IN APACHE PASS

George Nicholas Bascom graduated from West Point Military Academy and was appointed Lieutenant on July 1, 1858. After service in the Utah Expedition of 1859 he was transferred to Arizona and stationed at Fort Buchanan.

Leaving the Fort at the end of January, Bascom and his men followed the trail of the raiders, and on 3 February reached the

Overland Stage station at Apache Pass next to which Cochise was known to camp peacefully.

The following day the Chiricahua Apache leader and some of his band were invited to parley; as soon as they were in his tent, Bascom had soldiers encircle the camp and flatly accused Cochise of kidnapping the boy.

Cochise (truthfully, as it transpired) denied responsibility for either the raid or the kidnapping, but offered to try and get Felix back from the tribe holding him. Bascom refused to believe him and told Cochise he would be held hostage until the boy was returned, whereupon Cochise burst through the cordon and escaped, leaving three of his people prisoner.

Within twenty-four hours Cochise had taken four white men prisoner, and offered to trade them for his relatives. Bascom refused to countenance this unless the boy was returned, which Cochise could not do. Into this impasse rode another detachment led by Assistant Surgeon Bernard Irwin, bringing with them three Apache prisoners taken en route.

When on 14 February another body of troops arrived and heavy fighting commenced, Cochise killed his white prisoners, whereupon Irwin decided to execute the Apache prisoners in reprisal. When Bascom hesitated, Irwin told him he intended to hang his own prisoners anyway, whereupon Bascom capitulated and all six Apaches were executed.

The result of this atrocity was that Cochise embarked upon a war of attrition that would terrorize the Southwest for more than a decade.

The unfortunate young George Bascom has been blamed for igniting this conflict, but it does seem apparent that Irwin, who outranked him, was the true culprit.

In spite of this, Irwin was later awarded the Congressional Medal of Honour for gallantry in action on these two days, and retired with full honours in 1894, whereas Bascom was transferred to New Mexico, rising to the rank of captain just four months before he was killed in the Civil War battle of Valverde on 21 February, 1862.

Felix Tellez, the boy who had been kidnapped, reappeared later as Mickey Free, a scout for the US Army in the 1880s. It had not been Cochise's people who captured him but a band of Western Apaches.

Within two months of the Bascom debacle, more than 150 non-Apache men were killed as Mangas Coloradas and Cochise combined forces to attack miners, outlying camps and even small detachments of soldiers. they even ambushed General James Carleton's powerful California Column in Apache Pass in 1862, soon after the outbreak of the Civil War, although their attack was unsuccessful.

In 1863 Mangas Coloradas was captured near Pinos Altos and held prisoner at old Fort McLane, south of Silver City. Shortly thereafter, according to US Army records, he was 'killed while trying to escape,' but the consensus of history is that he was murdered when he angrily tried to fight off soldiers who were jabbing heated bayonets into his legs. Perhaps even more than Bascom's blunder, Mangas's death ignited the bloody, relentless Apache Wars which would rage for another quarter of a century, eventually costing well over four thousand lives.

After the last spike of the transcontinental Railroad was driven at Promontory, Utah, the locomotives of the Central Pacific and the Union Pacific Railroads were moved forward until pilots touched and locomotives were christened with bottles of wine and champagne. Shaking hands in the centre are chief engineers Montague and Dodge.

CHAPTER FOUR

COWTOWNS AND GUNSMOKE

O N 10 MAY 1869 an event that General William Tecumseh Sherman prophesied would 'bring the Indian problem to a final solution' took place north of the Great Salt Lake at Promontory Summit, Utah: the completion of the transcontinental railroad. Four celebratory spikes, replicas of the kind that actually held down the rails – two gold, one silver and one a blend of gold, silver and iron – were gently tapped into position (they would later be displayed in museums). Then a fifth, ordinary iron spike was hammered into place by Leland Stanford, formally joining the west-east Central Pacific railroad of which he was president and the east-west Union Pacific railroad into one continuous entity – the Union Pacific.

'Gold, Silver and Other Miners!' its advertising flyers screamed, 'Now is the time to seek your Fortunes in Nebraska, Wyoming, Arizona, Washington, Dakotah, Colorado, Utah, Oregon, Montana, New Mexico, Idaho, Nevada or California!' And they came, fortune seekers and sodbusters, adventurers and vagrants, fighting men and fools. More now than ever before, America was moving west. Even as the Union Pacific line was completed, its eastern division, renamed the Kansas Pacific, was already spearing across the plains toward Denver, Colorado. From Topeka, Kansas another line, the

Atchison, Topeka and Santa Fe, was aiming southwest toward Santa Fe and down the valley of the Rio Grande to El Paso, Texas. Others would follow: Northern Pacific, Denver Pacific, Texas and Pacific, Denver and Rio Grande, Burlington and Missouri.

The workers hired to build these lines were a tough, rowdy crew, many of them Irish, men who lived hard, drank hard and needed feeding a good square meal three times a day. The further west they built, the more difficult became the logistics of shipping food to them (the first refrigerated railroad car was not built until 1869). A solution was quickly found. Out there on the endless plains were millions and millions of buffalo, prime meat on the hoof. All the railroad builders needed to do was hire men to go out and kill them and bring in the meat and the problem was solved. Pretty soon buffalo hunting had become a full-time occupation and many famous frontiersmen made it their living, among them Wild Bill Hickok, Pat Garrett, Wyatt Earp, Bat Masterson and a young fellow named William F. Cody, who alone killed something like six thousand animals in the year 1867 while supplying the Union Pacific crews with meat and in the process earned himself the nickname 'Buffalo Bill'.

Thus the need to feed the graders and surveyors, the section gangs, the navvies and the gandy dancers and then the buffalo hide trade which followed became factors more significant than any battle, more damaging than any war or any disease the white man had visited upon the native American tribes. A further step in the eventual containment of all the native American tribes was made in 1871 when Congress passed the Indian Appropriation Act, which nullified all existing treaties with the Indians and made every single one of them national wards.

Although the United States Government never made any formal comment on the wholesale slaughter of the buffalo herds, its implicit approval may be presumed from the fact that it never made any effort to contain or control it. This, too, was Manifest Destiny: depriving the Indians of their principal food supply would (and did) force them into increasing and finally total dependency on the beef distributed on the reservations – which was exactly what the Army wanted.

The buffalo were, and had always been, the staple of life to the Indian tribes who lived there. Their tipis were made of buffalo hides, as were their clothes and moccasins. They ate buffalo meat. Their containers, their ropes, the bridles for their horses were made of hide, other containers came from bladders or stomachs. Small bones made their needles, sinew their thread. Unlike the Indians, who only killed what they needed, however, the white man was literally exterminating the buffalo. At one time, it is estimated, there may have been as many as 30,000,000 buffalo roaming the plains of the trans-Mississippi West; by the late 1870s they would be virtually extinct.

Year after year the slaughter accelerated. In the East manufacturers had developed techniques and machinery for converting buffalo hides to soft leather for shoes, for belts, for carriage hoods, for cushions. Men who could use guns – and that was most men – did the arithmetic: if there were twenty million buffalo and a buffalo hide was worth three dollars, that meant $60,000,000 was wandering about out there waiting to be picked up. All you needed was the price of a buffalo gun and some cartridges – a total investment of maybe $100 that could net you twenty times that in as many weeks – big money in a time when a hired hand got paid a dollar a day.

The buffalo hunters altered their methods accordingly. Now only the hides were taken from the dead buffalo: the rest of the carcass was left to rot on the prairies. It was said that the Kansas Pacific was lined with buffalo carcasses on both sides for two hundred miles. The new railroads inching westward across Kansas provided an easy service for getting the hides to the eastern markets quickly and cheaply. In the year 1872–73, following the introduction of the new Sharps 50-90 calibre cartridge, the 'Big Fifty' that could drop a buffalo dead in its tracks, it was estimated something like 1,500,000 buffalo hides were sent east on the Kansas railroads alone. And right alongside them, part of a new and burgeoning industry, went thousands and thousands of Texas cattle on their way to the slaughterhouses of Kansas City and from there as prime beef steak to the dinner tables of the eastern cities.

Cut off from the pre-war markets Texas ranchers had established on the Gulf of Mexico by the Union blockade of southern ports during the Civil War, the number of cattle running wild in Texas had multiplied exponentially. By 1865, there were perhaps six million of them in the brush country around San Antonio, Corpus Christi and Laredo. Full grown steers sold for so little money it was hardly worth the expense of rounding the animals up and driving them to market.

As early as 1866, Charles Goodnight, the son of a dirt farmer who had served as a scout for the Texas Rangers during the war, had realized the only way to make any money with these unwanted cattle was to try to take them north to better markets, to the new Indian reservations where the Army had to feed the Indians, and to the booming mining towns where fresh beef brought a decent price. He enlisted the aid of Oliver Loving, a man nearly twice his own age who had taken Texas cattle north as far as Chicago before the war. Together they blazed a seven-hundred-mile trail from Texas to the new Indian reservation at Fort Sumner in New Mexico, then beyond that to the mining camps in Colorado, and later still as far as Wyoming.

But the real revolution in the cattle business began when a far-sighted entrepreneur named Joseph G. McCoy – the original 'real McCoy' – realized that if Texas cattle hitherto driven to Missouri or eastern Kansas could be brought to the new railhead towns springing up on the plains, they could be shipped directly by train to the huge eastern markets crying out for supplies of fresh meat. McCoy made a trip to St Louis to get backing for his scheme. The Missouri Pacific threw him out; the Union Pacific was no more than lukewarm, but the Hannibal and St. Joseph Railroad proved more positive, a reaction which resulted in Kansas City's displacing St Louis as the major market for Texas cattle.

In 1867, McCoy purchased the townsite of Abilene for $2,400, won over local opposition to Texas cattle, laid out stockyards and loading facilities, and built a hotel that could sleep eighty guests. After distributing handbills to dozens of towns in the southwest announcing the new facilities, he sent a stockman friend he had engaged down to Texas to persuade drovers to come to Abilene. Something like forty thousand cattle arrived that year; they would soon be followed by hundreds of thousands more.

Abilene was the first cattle town – 'cowtown' was the more frequently-used description – but there would be plenty of others, with names that still ring through the saga of their era in a litany of legend: Ellsworth, Newton, Wichita, Caldwell, Hays City, Ogallalla, Cheyenne and most memorably of all, Dodge City, the 'cowboy capital'. In each of them there were merchants and bankers and businessmen and decent families. And in every one of them, 'on the wrong side of the tracks', were the gamblers, saloon-keepers and whores in their false-front shacks, tent brothels and deadfall saloons waiting to separate the cowboys from the wages they had earned on the trail.

As each of these 'hell towns' rose to ascendancy and then collapsed into a bucolic backwater as the rails – and the cattle – moved on, a sort of boom-and-bust pattern emerged. The story of Abilene serves as well as any to illustrate its arc. After the first trail herds arrived, the town began to grow and kept growing. Where there had been a scattering of log huts and a few outlying farms, frame buildings began to appear. By 1870 there were no less than four hotels, ten boarding houses, five general stores and ten saloons.

With one or two exceptions they were all one-story high with that style peculiar to the frontier town – the false front, a wooden façade designed to fool the onlooker into believing the building was two stories high and doing nothing of the kind. The town's principal meeting place, favoured by the Texas ranchers and the local movers and shakers was The Drover's Cottage on Main Street. Built by Joseph McCoy and run by J. W. Gore and his wife, it was three stories high with a hundred rooms, with an adjacent barn that could hold a hundred horses and fifty carriages if need be.

At first, the cowboys who came in with the herds virtually took over the town, riding from saloon to saloon (no self-respecting cowboy ever walked across a street) wide-brimmed Stetson hat thrown back, the two or three inch diameter rowels of their big Mexican spurs jingling, a Colt .45 revolver or some similar firearm holstered on their right hip. After maybe three months on the trail with only cows for company they were ready to have a rip-snorting, hell-raising time aimed at eating up every cent they had earned on the drive in the shortest possible time. Their order of priorities was simple: get cleaned up, get laid, and get drunk. They drank their liquor straight and were prone to settling their arguments with bullets (no self-respecting cowboy ever fought with his fists). And waiting for them – and their cash – was the cowtown, an oasis of pleasure in the drab landscape of the cowboy's life.

Although the cowtowns were nothing like as violent as myth has painted them – for instance, nobody was killed in Abilene during its first two years – there was an absence of law and order; the only way 'decent citizens' could contain the worst excesses and 'tame' the cowboys was to employ men known to be 'man-killers', gunfighters with the reputation of being ready to shoot first and ask questions later, men whose mere appearance on the scene could avert an impending gunfight or quell a drunken mob. These city marshals – town police chiefs, not to be confused with United States marshals – walked a fine line between keeping the unruly element in line and keeping the merchants and saloon-keepers who fed off them happy. Some of the town tamers were fine men, honest, brave. Others were no better than they had to be, and a few would in any modern assessment instantly be labelled as psychopaths. Their lives have been portrayed again and again in print and in countless films, on radio and television – more often than not inaccurately.

Men like Wyatt Earp and his brothers Morgan and Virgil, for instance, who moved from Wichita to Dodge City and then on to Tombstone, Arizona. Men like Wild Bill Hickok, who kept the law in Hays and Abilene; and others like the Masterson brothers, Henry Brown, Mike Meagher, Billy Tilghman, Bear River Tom Smith, 'Mysterious Dave' Mather and Charlie Bassett. It was men like these who gave birth to the modem legend of the gunfighter, the lone lawman going out to meet the killer on the dusty street at high noon. That it never happened is irrelevant: as one historian perspicaciously observed, if enough people are prepared to believe something, true or false, it's a fact.

Abilene got its first taste of law and order in September, 1869, when an ordinance was passed by the town council making it illegal to carry a deadly weapon inside the city limits. Signs prominently posted were very quickly shot to pieces by the very cowboys who were supposed to obey them. When a jail was built, they tore it down. When a black cook from one of the cattle camps was thrown into the rebuilt jail, they stormed it, delivered their cook, and trashed the town for the hell of it.

Abilene needed law, the city fathers decreed, and they hired it in the shape of 'Bear River' Tom Smith, who had won his nickname in a famous mining country battle. Perhaps uniquely among the town tamers, Smith preferred not to use the guns he carried, relying more often on his fists to enforce the law. Born in New York around 1830, he worked as a teamster for the Union Pacific railroad in Nebraska, and later at boom-and-bust Bear River City, Wyoming, where he became that town's first law officer.

Right away Smith enforced the ordinance against carrying guns in town, continuing to quell disturbances with his fists, often disarming an opponent and then 'buffaloing' him – i.e., relieving the miscreant of his gun and knocking him unconscious with it or using his own gun for the same purpose. That he was effective is indicated by the fact that on 4 August, the town council raised his salary from the original $150 a month to $225. On 8 September, it was reported he had also closed down the red light district south of the railroad tracks – the 'wrong' side – in what they called 'Texas Town', a single street packed with saloons, gambling houses and brothels. Although he took a tough line, Smith killed no one in the five months he policed Abilene.

Then on 23 October, 1870, in a fatal affray on Chapman Creek, about ten miles (16km) from Abilene, one Andrew McConnell killed a neighbour, John Shea. Another neighbour, Moses Miles, confirmed to the court that McConnell had acted in self-defence, and he was freed. A week or so later, however, it transpired Miles's testimony was perjured and city marshal Tom Smith and his deputy Jim McDonald (acting for the Sheriff, who was too ill to make the arrest himself) went down to McConnell's dugout on 2 November to arrest him. When they got there Miles was present. As Smith read the warrant, McConnell shot him through the chest. Although mortally wounded, Smith in turn shot McConnell and as the two men wrestled with each other McDonald fled the scene, whereupon Miles clubbed Tom Smith to the ground with his gun, then picked up an axe and all but decapitated the lawman. The killers were captured a few days later, tried the following March, and sent to prison, McConnell for twelve and Miles for sixteen years. The remains of Tom Smith, buried at the time in a two-dollar grave, were disinterred in 1904 and marked by an imposing monument saluting him as 'A Fearless Hero of Frontier Days Who in Cowboy Chaos Established the Supremacy of Law'.

Abilene's next marshal was Patrick Hand, a gunsmith; he was replaced by Smith's deputy, James McDonald. Before long, to quote the Abilene Chronicle, 'every principle of right and justice was at a discount. No man's life or property was safe from the murderous intent and lawless invasions of Texans.' With the opening of a new cattle season imminent the city fathers decided to fill the law-enforcement vacuum caused by Tom Smith's death by bringing in the most famous gunfighter of his day, James Butler 'Wild Bill' Hickok. 'The law-abiding citizens decided upon a change, and it was thought best to fight the devil with his own weapons,' said the Chronicle. 'Accordingly, Marshal Hickok, known as 'Wild Bill,' was elected marshal.'

'WILD BILL', THE PRINCE OF PISTOLEERS

James Butler Hickok began his life on 27 May, 1837 on a farm in Homer (later Troy Grove) Illinois. At nineteen he joined James H. Lane's Free State Army in Kansas and served for a year, reportedly as the general's bodyguard. Already becoming known for his skill with firearms, he was elected Constable of Monticello, Kansas, in March 1858, but left later that year and hired out as a teamster with the famous firm of Russell, Majors and Waddell. While assigned to Rock Spring Station, Nebraska, he was involved in a 12 July, 1861 fight with David McCanles in which McCanles and two other men were killed, an encounter magnified beyond recognition in a

Harper's Magazine article by George Ward Nichols (later Hickok's biographer) that made 'Wild Bill' nationally famous.

During the Civil War Hickok served as a wagon-master, scout, sharpshooter and spy; there are almost as many legends as facts about his adventures during this period. At war's end Hickok settled in Springfield, Missouri where, on 21 July 1865 he killed Davis Tutt in a duel that took place in the town's main square. The following year he was at Fort Riley, Kansas, where he worked as a scout and guide and also served as deputy US Marshal.

He became acquainted with General George A. Custer at Fort Riley, Kansas, where he served as a deputy US marshal and is said to have been a scout for General W. S. Hancock's campaign against the Plains Indians in 1867.

By the time he became Sheriff of Ellis County, Kansas, at a special election in August 1869, 'dime novels' describing his fictional adventures were encouraging would-be badmen to test him. In August 1869 he killed a cavalryman named Bill Mulvey, and the following month a teamster named Samuel Strawhun. Both killings were considered justified. The following year he killed a soldier, John Kile, and wounded another in a saloon fight in Hays City and hastily quit that locality.

On 15 April, 1871 he became Marshal of Abilene where, on 5 October, 1871, while breaking up a drunken brawl outside the Alamo saloon, he mortally wounded gambler Phil Coe. During the shootout a man ran between the opponents brandishing a pistol and the edgy Hickok killed him, too. Later it was discovered the man was Mike Williams, a special policeman hired by the Novelty Theatre to keep the Texans away from the dancers. It is a matter of record that Hickok never fired his gun at another man again as long as he lived.

He capitalized on his fame by appearing, briefly, in Buffalo Bill's Wild West Show. He settled in Cheyenne, Wyoming, guiding hunting parties; although for obvious reasons he kept it quiet, he was going blind. On 5 March 1876 he married Agnes Lake. After their honeymoon he joined a mining party going to Deadwood, South Dakota. There, on 2 August 1876, he was shot in the back of the head by Jack McCall; the cards he was holding – black aces, black eights, and the jack of diamonds – have ever since been known as the 'Dead Man's Hand'.

How many men did he kill? According to his biographer, Hickok himself claimed 'only thirty- six'. That 'only' alone would seem to entitle him to his reputation.

At the end of the 1871 cattle season, Abilene decided it no longer needed the expensive services of the Prince of Pistoleers, and accordingly on 13 December Wild Bill was dismissed as city marshal. His services were no longer required: the railroad had moved on and so had the trail drives. From 1871–73 the hell-on-wheels towns were Ellsworth, to the west of Abilene and simultaneously Newton, to the south. Their brief and murderous notoriety was in turn eclipsed by a newer, bigger, raunchier and deadlier boom town that sprang up in the year 1870 under the supervision of Joseph G. McCoy and was for two years the head-quarters of the cattle trade.

Its name was Wichita and by November, 1870, it had 175 buildings and a population of nearly eight hundred. Among the early arrivals were a 'family' that consisted of homesteader William Antrim and a widow named Catherine McCarty and her two sons, Joe and Henry. Mrs McCarty would be remembered for operating a hand laundry on North Main Street; her son Henry would change his name to William H. Bonney and later become the legendary 'Billy the Kid.'

Wichita's residents at this time were, to cite a newspaper of the time:

Broad-brimmed and spurred Texans, keen business men, real estate agents, land seekers, greasers [a pejorative term of the period for anyone of Mexican descent], hungry lawyers, gamblers, women with white sun bonnets and shoes of a certain pattern, express wagons going pell mell, prairie schooners, farm wagons, and all rushing after the almighty dollar. The cattle season has not yet fully set in, but there is a rush of gamblers and harlots who are 'lying in wait' for the game which will soon begin to come up from the south. There was a struggle for a while who should run the city, the hard cases or the better people. The latter got the mastery, and have only kept it by holding a 'tight grip.' Pistols are as thick as blackberries.

The taxes are paid by the money received from whiskey sellers, gambling hells, and the demi monde, and thousands of dollars are obtained besides to further the interests of the town. [The town] flourishes off the cattle business, and these evils have to be put up with; at least that is the way a large majority of the people see it. But notwithstanding this a man is as safe [here] as anywhere else if he keeps out of bad company. The purlieus of crime there are no worse than in many eastern cities of boasted refinement and good order. But woe to the 'greeny' [greenhorn, i.e., tenderfoot] who falls into the hands of the dwellers therein, especially if he carries money. From these must come most of the stories of outrage at Wichita. They are entitled to little sympathy because they can find plenty of good company if they desire it.

As Wichita grew, luxuriously-appointed hotels sprang up – the

Occidental, the Douglas Avenue and the Texas House – and the saloons multiplied like mushrooms; here as in the other cowtowns, there was a 'proper' town on one side of the river – in this instance the Arkansas River – and on the other, the 'addition' which was called Delano. Prominent among the latter's notable badmen was a gunman-gambler named Rowdy Joe Lowe who, with his 'wife' Kate, kept 'the swiftest joint in Kansas'. Joe and Kate had also run saloons in Ellsworth and Newton, where Joe had been indicted for crimes such as robbery, theft, and operating a house of prostitution, and then killing a man named Sweet in the latter town after Sweet made a pass at Kate. Usually, however, Rowdy Joe kept order his own way: if one of his customers got too rambunctious, Joe would calm him down by beating him about the head and face with a pistol.

Delano's other hard man – who apparently loathed Rowdy Joe as enthusiastically as Rowdy Joe loathed him – was Edward T. 'Red' Beard, who operated a dance-hall saloon next door to Joe's. It was in this establishment on 3 June 1873 that a cavalryman from nearby Fort Hays got into a fight with Emma Stanley, one of Red's girls, and shot her in the thigh, whereupon Red Beard pulled his gun and started firing indiscriminately. When the smoke cleared, a soldier named Doley (not the one who had started the trouble) was dead and two others seriously wounded.

Two days later the soldiers came back in force, some thirty of them intent on avenging their dead comrade. They put a cordon around Sheriff John Meagher's house to prevent his intervention, then a squad marched to Red's saloon and set fire to it, in the process wounding a man named Charles Leshart and one of the saloon girls; Emma Stanley was also wounded yet again.

A little over four months later Red Beard got into a fight with Rowdy Joe while both of them were out of their skulls on ninety per cent proof alcohol. Some accounts say Red just marched into Joe's saloon and started shooting, others merely that they 'waltzed into a deadly melee.' Both carried shotguns; both started shooting. Joe was slightly wounded in the back of the neck, Red was blasted with buckshot in the arm and hip. Yet another dance-hall girl, Annie Franklin, took a bullet through the stomach and Bill Anderson – who had himself killed a man 'by mistake' the preceding spring in Wichita – was shot through the head. Beard died on 11 November. Rowdy Joe was tried and found not guilty of murder but when a further indictment was filed for the murder of Anderson he promptly departed for parts unknown.

Wichita would remain a tough town for some years to come – as would neighbouring Caldwell and Hays City – but a new star was rising in the west, an evil beacon that would shine undimmed for almost ten unapologetic and unregenerate years: the 'beautiful, bibulous Babylon' of the Kansas plains called Dodge City. First it was the railhead of the AT&SF, the 'hell on wheels' where the railroad's track crews spent their weekly wages, then it became the centre of the buffalo hunting and hide trade and finally, when the stockyards were completed in 1875, the greatest and longest-lived of all the cowtowns.

Dodge was still a buffalo hunter's town in 1872 when Billy Brooks, oftentimes called 'Bully' and a former city marshal of Newton, got into an argument with a Santa Fe railroad yardmaster named Brown. Both pulled guns and started firing; one of Brown's bullets wounded Brooks, but Brooks's third shot killed Brown on the spot. Just five days later, on 28 December, following his falling out with Dodge saloonkeeper Matthew Sullivan, someone – it was widely believed to have been Brooks – poked a gun through the window of Sullivan's saloon and shot him dead. After another fight with a buffalo hunter the following March in which he barely escaped with his life, Brooks sought pastures new. He is said to have been hanged by vigilantes in Caldwell a couple of years later.

Pretty soon Dodge had a population of about a thousand, most of them subsisting on the buffalo trade, which in 1873 generated 1,617,000 pounds of meat, 2,743,100 pounds of bones (for making fertilisers) and 459,453 hides. Then in 1875 the trail herds began arriving in Dodge, diverted by the barbed wire being strung across the plains by settlers. Over the next two years Dodge City expanded to welcome them. A fifty room hotel, the Dodge House, offering a daily menu of delicacies and imported wines, blossomed on Front Street. The famous Long Branch saloon opened further down, and across th e plaza the Lady Gay and Comique theatres were erected. Two more dance halls – one of them run by Rowdy Kate Lowe – were added to the four already operating. Ham Bell, former Marshal of Great Bend, built the Elephant, a livery stable so big it covered three city blocks.

And to them came the cowboys, young Texans by the hundred. The Santa Fe tracks were the 'deadline'. On the north side you minded your manners and checked your guns at one of the places designated by the law. South of the tracks, there were no rules: saloons, gambling houses and brothels never closed; pistol shots rang out throughout the day and night, sometimes in celebration, sometimes in anger. Dodge would give the world two generic names: the term 'red light district' came from The Red Light House, a brothel that stood south of the tracks, and the second, its cemetery which was dubbed 'Boot Hill' and spawned a hundred namesakes all the way across the West. Nobody knows for sure how many men died violently during Dodge's heyday. Robert L. Wright, an early mayor of the town, said there were twenty-five killings during the first year of the cattle drive and it may even be true. They told the story of a conductor on a train heading west asking a man where he was going. 'To Hell, I reckon,' the man said. 'Okay,' said the conductor, 'give me a dollar and get off at Dodge.'

But for all that, it was not the mythical Gunsmoke TV version of Dodge City featuring James Arness as Marshal Matt Dillon, his deputies (first Chester, then Festus), the crusty-but-benign Doc, feisty saloonkeeper Miss Kitty – and a stand-up, face-to-face, quick-draw gunfight once a week, every week.

To be sure, Dodge had more than its quotient of deadly gun-fighters. At one time or another Doc Holliday, Clay Allison, 'Mysterious Dave' Mather, Bat Masterson and his brothers Ed and Jim, Wyatt Earp and his brothers Morgan, Virgil and James, Luke Short, 'Longhaired' Jim Courtright, Billy Tilghman, 'Cockeyed Frank' Loving and Wild Bill Hickok patrolled its streets on one side of the law or the other. With such a volatile cast of characters around, perhaps what is surprising is not that there were gunfights, but that all things considered, there were so few.

DODGE CITY: THE GUNFIGHTS

Monday, 23 December 1872

Ex-stage driver and former marshal at Newton Billy Brooks gets into a quarrel with a Santa Fe yardmaster (also from Newton) named Brown. Each man fires three shots at the other. Brown's first shot wounds Brooks, but Brooks' third shot, after nicking one of Brown's assistants, kills the yardmaster on the spot.

Saturday, 28 December 1872

Matthew Sullivan, saloonkeeper, is shot dead by someone who fires into the saloon through an open window. Billy Brooks is widely believed to have been the assassin, but no action is taken against him.

Thursday, 4 March 1873

Billy Brooks comes under fire from a 'needle gun' wielded by a man named Jordan. He takes cover behind a water butt and escapes unhurt.

Tuesday, 25 September 1877

Riding his horse, a drunken cowboy named A. C. Jackson fires his gun into the air a few times outside Beatty and Kelley's saloon on Front Street, and Sheriff Bat Masterson orders him to surrender his gun. Jackson shouts refusal, fires his gun a couple more times and gallops off. Bat and his deputy brother Ed open fire, wounding the horse. The cowboy escapes.

Monday, 5 November 1877

During the afternoon, a quarrel erupts between Texas Dick Moore and Bob Shaw, owners of the Lone Star dance hall and saloon. The law is summoned. Assistant City Marshal Ed Masterson orders Shaw to surrender his weapon, but instead Shaw takes a shot at Moore. Masterson clubs Shaw over the head with his pistol but fails to put him down. Shaw opens fire on Masterson, who is hit in the right side of the chest, the bullet emerging through the shoulder-blade. His right arm paralysed, Masterson drops his gun. Snatching it up in his left hand, he puts one shot into Shaw's left arm and another in his left leg, knocking him off his feet. During the fight a random bullet hits Dick Moore in the groin and another wounds bystander Frank Buskirk. All the participants recover.

Tuesday, 9 April 1878

Keeping an eye on a noisy party of Texas cowboys in the Lady Gay dance hall, City Marshal Ed Masterson (promoted the preceding December) notices one of them, Jack Wagner, is carrying a pistol. At about ten p.m. he disarms Wagner and hands the gun to Wagner's boss, Alf Walker. When Masterson and his deputy Nat Haywood leave the saloon, Walker gives Wagner his gun back and the two of them follow the lawmen outside, where Masterson grapples with Wagner for possession of his gun. As Haywood tries to assist, Walker tries to shoot the deputy but his gun misfires; instead he and his cowboys hold him at bay with drawn guns.

Wagner jams his gun against Masterson's belly and fires. The flash sets Masterson's clothes on fire; the bullet tears through the lawman's body and comes out the back. In spite of this massive wound Masterson gets his gun out and fires four shots. One hits Wagner in the belly, the other three smash into Walker, one through the chest and the other two shattering his right arm. Two bystanders in the large crowd that has gathered are also slightly wounded by flying bullets.

Wagner staggers into Peacock's saloon and collapses on the floor; Walker rushes straight through the building and falls outside the rear door. Masterson, his clothes still smouldering, walks two hundred yards to George Hoover's saloon on the other side of the tracks, where he tells George Hinkle 'George, I'm shot,' before collapsing on the floor. Carried into his brother Bat Masterson's room at the rear of the saloon, he dies within half an hour. Wagner dies of his wound on 10 November.

Friday, 26 July 1878

At about three a.m some drunken Texas cowboys getting ready to leave town begin firing into the Comique Dance Hall, creating panic among the 150 or so revellers inside. Constables Wyatt Earp and Jim Masterson arrive on the scene and shots are exchanged. One cowboy, George Hoyt, is wounded in the arm; infection sets in and on 21 August he dies.

Saturday, 17 August 1878

Drunken cowboys attempt to take over the bar at the Comique. Policemen (probably Charlie Bassett, Jim Masterson and Wyatt Earp) bend a few heads with their six-guns and although shots are fired no one is seriously injured.

Friday, 4 October 1878

Resentful of rough treatment he had received at the hands of James 'Dog' Kelley, the mayor of Dodge City, who threw him out of his saloon, Texas cowboy Jim Kenedy – who had some years earlier nearly shot Print Olive to death in Newton – decide to assassinate Kelley. In the early hours of the morning he goes to Kelley's house and fires four shots into it. One of them hits and kills Fannie Keenan, a singer in shows at the Varieties and Comique who used the stage name Dora Hand. A posse led by Bat Masterson, now Sheriff of Ford County, that included Wyatt Earp, Billy Tilghman and Charlie Bassett pursue and next day catch up with Kenedy who puts up a fight in which his right arm is shattered and his horse killed. He was later unaccountably acquitted of the killing.

Saturday, 5 April 1879

Gambler 'Cockeyed Frank' Loving and freighter Levi Richardson are in dispute over a woman. This Saturday night Richardson is about to leave the Long Branch saloon when Loving comes in and takes a seat at a gambling table. Richardson also sits down at the table and in moments the two are on their feet shouting insults at each other. Both men draw their guns, Richardson firing first and missing. Loving's gun misfires and he runs behind a stove as Richardson fires two more shots. Loving then begins firing and Richardson is hit in the chest, side and right arm. Still firing his own gun he falls back against a table, and bystander William Duffy grabs the gun to stop the fight. The action is unnecessary; Richardson is dead within minutes, Loving's only injury is a scratch on the hand.

Monday, 9 June 1879

When a group of cowboys refuse to surrender their weapons on entering town, a couple of local lawmen (probably Wyatt Earp and Jim Masterson) get into a shooting affray in which one of the cowboys is shot in the leg as the rest gallop out of town.

Saturday, 9 April 1881

Jim Masterson and A. J. Peacock, co-owners of the Lady Gay saloon and dance hall, get into a quarrel, aggravated by an employee, bartender Al Updegraff who supports Peacock. All three start shooting but no one is hurt and the quarrel is (temporarily) patched up.

Saturday, 16 April 1881

Following receipt of a telegram from his brother describing his difficulties with Updegraff, Bat Masterson arrives in Dodge by train from New Mexico. As he alights he sees Peacock and Updegraff across the street and shouts 'I have come over a thousand miles to settle this. I know you are heeled – now fight!'. Although the street is crowded, all three draw their guns and begin firing, Masterson from behind the railway embankment, Updegraff and Peacock from the jail.

As the bullets fly, two more men (probably Jim Masterson and Charlie Ronan) join the fight, firing from a nearby saloon. Although it is not known who fires the shot, Updegraff is shot through the chest and a fleeing bystander slightly wounded. The fight is then stopped by Mayor A. B. Webster and Sheriff Fred Singer. After paying a small fine Bat Masterson leaves town accompanied by his brother and Ronan.

30 April 1883

Three female 'singers' working at the Long Branch saloon owned by Will Harris and gambler Luke Short were arrested, much to Short's annoyance. Meeting city clerk L. C. Hartman (who as special constable had helped make the arrests) on Front Street, Short pulls a gun and fires twice at Hartman, who hits the dirt. Thinking Hartman dead, Short turns and walks away, whereupon Hartman fires a shot at the retreating gambler. His misses, too.

Sunday, 6 July 1884

Following some serious provocation, gambler Dave St. Clair shoots and kills Bing Choate, who has just boasted, six-shooter in hand, that he is 'the fastest sonofabitch in town.'

Friday, 18 July 1884

In a fight which breaks out near the Opera House, assistant Marshal Tom Nixon tries to shoot at ex-Marshal Dave Mather. Although the shot misses, it is fired near enough to powder-burn Mather's face. The cause of the fight is said to have been 'an old feud'.

Monday, 21 July 1884

At about 10 p.m. Tom Nixon, 'on duty' at the corner of Front Street and First Avenue is shot dead on the spot by Mather, who comes downstairs from his saloon in the Opera House, tells Nixon 'You have lived long enough,' then fires four times without warning. A cowboy named Archie Franklin standing nearby is wounded in the leg by one of the bullets which passed through Nixon's body. When arrested, Mather says 'I ought to have killed him months ago.' The cause of the fight is believed to have been Nixon's part in getting a saloon operated by Mather closed. The following year, after a change of venue, Mather is found not guilty of murder and walks free.

Tuesday, 16 October 1884

At about ten p.m. Marshal Billy Tilghman confronts a rowdy bunch of cowboys near the toll bridge over the Arkansas River and when they pull their guns, empties his pistol at them. 'About twenty five or thirty' shots are fired, but when Billy switches to a Winchester, the boys fire a couple more defiant shots then gallop off unhurt.

Sunday, 10 May 1885

In an argument that blows up over a penny-ante card game in the Junction saloon, bullets fly as Dave Mather (or perhaps his brother, Josiah, the bartender at the saloon) shoots and kills David Barnes, is himself slightly wounded in the head while John Wall is hit in the leg and C. C. Camp shot through both legs. Further casualties are avoided when Sheriff Pat Sughrue breaks up the fight, grabbing Barnes's brother John as he tries to get his gun out and also arresting Josiah Mather, Dave Mather's brother. Neither ever stands trial: they both skip town, forfeiting their bonds. Dave Mather remains 'Mysterious' to the end: the date, place and manner of his death remain unknown.

In 1885 and 1886 a series of fires destroyed most of Dodge City, but it was not the fires that tamed the town, it was the steady, relentless influx of settlers drawn by the availability of free land made by Congress twenty years earlier in the Homestead Act of 1862, which promised 160 acres of public land to anyone who filed a claim, paid a ten-dollar fee and agreed to work the property for five years. It had been thought at first that settlers could not live on what Major Stephen Long had once dubbed 'the Great American Desert,' but the late 1870s and the early 80s were unusually wet years in the West, with the result that bumper crops were reaped everywhere the ground had been broken.

At first, most of those who came were farmers from the midwestern states, but it was not until the railroad companies, desperate for passenger traffic, sent agents to Europe to recruit settlers that the great exodus began. Between 1863 and 1890 nearly one million people filed homestead applications. A growing stream of Jewish, Swedish, Dutch, German, French, English and Irish families began to arrive on the plains, bringing with them the windmill, the plough, the sod house and – death to the open range – barbed wire. Soon over 100,000 acres of Ford County were under cultivation, nearly 20,000 of them fenced. Domestic cattle took the place of longhorns, winter wheat that of prairie grass. While the days of the trail drive were not yet quite over, the day of the homesteader – sodbusters, as the cowboys pityingly called them – had come. And they had come to stay.

American outlaw William Bonney (1859–1881), better known
as Billy the Kid.

CHAPTER FIVE

TO THE LAST MAN

THE FACT THAT THEY HAD the right to file on homestead land and begin farming did not mean that
homesteaders were welcomed everywhere with open
arms – in fact, in many places the angry opposite was very much
the case. When a man put his brand on the land he put it there for
good: possession in these circumstances was ninety-nine points of
the law. Let someone try to take it from him – no matter how legally
– and there would be war.

By the 1880s, many of the cattlemen who had once herded half-
wild longhorn steers up the long and dangerous trails to eastern
markets had become sophisticated breeders of pedigree cattle providing the higher quality beef now in demand. Men like Charles
Goodnight in Texas, Alexander Swan in Wyoming or John Chisum
in New Mexico owned – by right of possession and determination
(backed by a force of well-armed cowboys) – vast tracts of land on
which their stock roamed and which they were considerably less
than willing to let homesteaders file upon. The economics of the
cattle industry required the open range to remain open. The arithmetic was simple: each cow needed up to ten acres of open range –
and access to water – to thrive. A herd of eighty to a hundred thousand head of cattle required anywhere between half a million and a

million acres to forage upon. As a result, its owners would strenu-
ously oppose the incursion of settlers of any kind, and especially
'nesters' who would fence off water, build houses, and if and when
times got hard – which for nesters they frequently did – turn to
stealing cattle for food or money or both.

As a result feuds – sometimes called 'wars' – flared, in Montana
between cattlemen and nesters, in New Mexico between cattle-
owning businessmen seeking to maintain their monopoly of army
beef contracts and newcomers trying to unseat them; in Arizona
between cattlemen and sheepmen, and in Texas between warring
families – feuds that went on for so long that the men fighting them
were never entirely sure what had started them in the first place.
One such was the Sutton–Taylor feud, the longest and bloodiest of a
dozen or more in Texas history, which grew out of the period
between 1865 and 1877 known in the South as 'Reconstruction.'

A major problem facing the nation after the Civil War was the
restoration of the devastated economy of the defeated South. Controversy arose over the conditions under which States which had
seceded might be readmitted to the Union. As a first step in this
process, Congress divided the South into military districts under the
control of Federal troops. The Army ensured its control of the
southern states (many southerners were disqualified from voting
because of their wartime activities, while black men were not only
given the vote but also the right to hold office) by installing carpetbaggers, scalawags and former slaves in political offices; in five
southern states black men held a majority of the seats in the state
legislature. Concluding they could never get justice in this 'black dic-
tatorship' southerners responded by organizing secret societies such
as the Ku Klux Klan to keep the blacks 'in their place.'

In Texas, carpetbaggers (financial adventurers from the north so
called because it was said they could carry all they owned in a single

valise) had flooded in. Edmund J. Davis, who became Governor and virtual dictator of Texas at this time, was one of them, 'elected by popular ballot' in 1870 to administer what was hatingly referred to throughout the state as the Carpetbag Constitution. No more bitter controversy marked Davis's regime than his establishment of a state militia and a state police force, both to be answerable to him.

Many Texans, who perceived them as having been created solely to enforce 'carpetbagger law' hated the state police as the devil hates holy water, none more fiercely than John Wesley Hardin, who killed two black state policemen in Gonzales later that year. In his autobiography Hardin depicted the force as:

> *Carpetbaggers, scalawags from the north [Democrats who had turned their political coats in order to get into office] with ignorant Negroes frequently on the force. Instead of protecting life, liberty and property, they frequently destroyed it. We knew that many members of the State Police outfit were members of some secret vigilante gang, especially in DeWitt and Gonzales counties. We were all opposed to mob law and so soon became bitter enemies.*

JOHN WESLEY HARDIN

Although never as celebrated a shootist as (say) Wild Bill Hickok, John Wesley (Wes) Hardin was probably one of the greatest man-killers of them all. The son of James Gibson and Elizabeth (Dixon) Hardin, he was born in Bonham, Texas, on 26 May 1853. His father was a Methodist preacher, circuit rider, schoolteacher, and lawyer. Highly partisan Southern sympathies and a deeply-ingrained hatred for blacks motivated Hardin's violent career, which is said to have started in 1867 with a schoolyard squabble in which he stabbed and wounded another youth, albeit not fatally. He was only fifteen when he shot and killed a former slave known as Mage (short for Major Holzhausen) who – Hardin claimed – had threatened to kill him.

With the law (or in Hardin's eyes what passed for law) in Texas looking for him, he fled to his aunt's house, twenty-five miles north of Sumpter, Texas, where in the fall of 1868 he is said to have killed three Union soldiers who sought to arrest him for the murder of Mage. The following summer, he and his cousin Simp Dixon, a member of the Ku Klux Klan with a price on his head, ran into a squad of soldiers near Pisgah, and in the ensuing shootout killed one man each. On Christmas Day, 1869, Hardin killed Jim Bradley, a Towash gambler who had tried to cheat him. The following month at Horn Hill he got into another fight, this time with a circus worker, and killed him, too. Unbelievably, that same January he killed Alan Comstock, who mistook him for a 'rube' and tried to enmesh Wes in a badger game. Hardin was captured and arrested by State Police Lieutenant E. T. Stokes and Officer Jim Smolly. On the way back to Waco to be tried, Hardin killed Smolly and escaped.

In 1871 Hardin linked up with his cousins the Clements brothers, and went up the Chisholm Trail as a cowboy with Jim Clements. In his 'autobiography' he claimed to have killed five 'Mexicans' and two Indians in fights en route and three more in Abilene, Kansas, after allegedly facing down city marshal Wild Bill Hickok, who Hardin says gave him the nickname 'Little Arkansas.'

Returning to Texas, Hardin soon got into difficulties again with two State Policemen who tried to arrest him in Nopal, killing one of them and severely wounding the other. Hardin also claimed to have killed three more of a posse of black men that came after him. If true, it would mean that by September, 1871 the 18-year old Texan had already killed twenty-seven men, 'a fair-sized cemetery' as his biographer puts it. It is clear that even this early in his life Hardin had a hair-trigger temper, a taste for hard liquor and cards, and as much compunction as a rattlesnake when it came to killing a man.

On 29 February 1872 John Wesley Hardin married 14-year-old storekeeper's daughter Jane Bowen. It wasn't much of a marriage – Hardin was a seriously absentee husband – but out of it came a son and two daughters, Mary Elizabeth the firstborn in 1873, John Wesley Jr in 1875 and Jane 'Jennie' in 1877.

Early in August, 1872 at Trinity City, Hardin added the name of Phil Sublett to his list of victims and was himself wounded in the gunfight. He killed another State Police officer who came after him and was again wounded before surrendering to Cherokee County Sheriff Richard Reagan in September 1872; as he was surrendering his guns a deputy, misreading his intention, wounded him in the leg. Incarcerated at Austin, he broke jail in October and began stock raising but was soon 'in' with the boys again, drinking, shooting at targets and racing horses at Nopal. The following April, after a barroom argument, he killed an Irishman named Morgan in Cuero and rode out of town unchecked.

Drawn into the Sutton–Taylor Feud in 1873–74, Hardin tried to hedge his bets for a while, but finally aligned himself with the Taylor camp. Late in July 1873, he and Jim Taylor killed the opposition leader, Jack Helm, a former State Police captain who had been dismissed following charges of brutality and embezzlement, yet had somehow become Sheriff of DeWitt County. In effect, this promoted Hardin to leadership of the Taylor faction.

As well as gambling and racing horses, Hardin was now dealing widely in stolen cattle, with his lawyer brother Joe taking care of all the paperwork. In late May, 1874 he, Jim Taylor and Bill Dixon killed Charles Webb, deputy sheriff of Brown County in a gunfight at Comanche. The wounded Hardin and his pals were saved from a lynching only by the intervention of local Sheriff John Carnes.

From that time, Hardin was constantly pursued in Texas. Following the lynching of his brother Joe, two of Bill Dixon's brothers and a number of other Taylor sympathizers, and with a price of $4000 on his head, dead or alive, he took his wife and children to Florida and Alabama, adding one certain and five more possible victims – among them Pinkerton detectives and brawlers in a Mobile gambling house – to his death list before lawmen captured him following a shootout in the smoking car of a train en route to Pensacola, Florida, on 23 July 1877.

Hardin was tried at Comanche for the murder of Charles Webb and sentenced, on 28 September 1878, to twenty-five years in jail. During his prison term he made repeated efforts to escape, read theological books, was superintendent of the prison Sunday school, and studied law. He was pardoned on 16 March 1894, and shortly thereafter admitted to the State bar.

In 1895 – his wife Jane had died before Hardin got out of the penitentiary – he married a teenager, Carolyn 'Callie' Lewis (some stories suggest he won her in a poker game) but after a couple of weeks he returned her to her parents. Hardin went to El Paso where he established a law practice. Despite efforts to lead a decent life, he was soon in trouble, drinking and gambling – unsuccessfully. He took as his lover Beulah, the wife of one of his clients, Martin M'rose, and when M'rose – a wanted man hiding out in Juarez, Mexico – found out about the affair, Hardin conspired with US deputy Marshal George Scarborough and others to get M'Rose to come across the river, where they assassinated him.

Hardin's life deteriorated still further when Beulah left him. He was drinking heavily and deeply in debt. On 19 August 1895, claiming Hardin had threatened to shoot him on sight (others hinted darkly it was because Hardin had not paid him for the killing of M'Rose, in which Selman had also been involved), Constable John Selman walked into the Acme Saloon where Hardin was playing dice with a friend and shot him three times. Hardin died instantly and was buried in Concordia Cemetery, El Paso.

*

On Easter Sunday of the following year, John Selman was himself killed by, of all people, George Scarborough. Hardin's autobiography, completed to the beginning of his law studies in prison, was published the same year. In it Hardin depicted himself as a pillar of society, always maintaining that he never killed anyone who did not need killing and that he only ever got into shooting situations to save his own life. Many people who knew him or his family regarded him as a man more sinned against than sinning. Simply put, he was a violent product of a violent time. But one thing is certain: no more dangerous, no more unpredictable gunfighter ever lived than 'Little Arkansas.'

THE TAYLOR–SUTTON FEUD

By the time Wes Hardin became embroiled in it, the Taylor–Sutton feud had been ablaze for some years. There is a persistent legend, probably begun by early-day journalists, that the two families had feuded elsewhere, but absolutely no evidence has ever been adduced to support it. In fact, the origins of the feud are still swathed in uncertainty and controversy. The Taylor clan, composed of largely unrepentant Confederates, was led by patriarch Josiah Taylor, a Virginian who settled near Cuero in DeWitt County (about halfway between San Antonio and the Gulf Coast) together with his five sons, Pitkin, Creed, Josiah, William and Rufus Taylor, with their sons, nephews, in-laws, and friends.

The opposing faction were relatives or followers of William E. Sutton, a native of Fayette County who had also moved to DeWitt County. To the public at large, the Taylors were perceived as stock thieves or rustlers, while the Suttons – despite their brutal methods

– were seen as embattled vigilante/lawmen. The rules of engagement were brutally simple: in a feud, anyone who harmed a
member of your clan harmed you. Whatever method achieved
revenge, whatever means was employed to remove a dangerous
enemy was acceptable, even praiseworthy.

Some believe the trouble between the two clans began in 1866
when Buck Taylor shot a black sergeant who came to a dance at
Taylor's uncle's home, and Hays Taylor killed a black soldier in an
Indianola saloon. In 'Reconstruction' Texas, killing a black man
meant certain conviction and death, especially if that black man was
a member of the hated Texas State Police: the names of two of Creed
Taylor's sons went automatically onto a 'Wanted' poster. Later, Hays
and another brother, Philip 'Doboy' Taylor, were involved in the
killing of two Yankee (read 'black') soldiers at Mason in November
1867. They were also accused of having killed two bounty hunters
who came after them, a crime which stirred the military commander, General Reynolds, to hire two heavies named C. S. Bell and
John Helm to go after Creed Taylor's boys.

Early in July 1869, at the head of a posse of about fifty men,
Helm arrived in the cattle country between DeWitt County and the
Gulf with the stated purpose of arresting rustlers. Prominent among
Helm's 'Regulators' during this purge were Joe Tumlinson and Jim
Cox, DeWitt County cattlemen. According to newspaper reports this
gang killed twenty-one men and arrested another ten between the
time of their arrival and the end of August; many of those killed
were shot 'trying to escape.' Not all of them were Taylors, of course,
but among them were family friends or relatives of the clan.

On 23 August 1869, another posse led by Bell laid an ambush
that resulted in the death of Hays Taylor. When on 1 July 1870 the
State Police force was established, Jack Helm became one of its four
captains and was sent back to the southeastern counties to continue

his 'war' on rustlers. Among those men he recruited were men like Cox, Tumlinson and Bill Sutton who had already demonstrated their loyalty to the cause; the rest were or would inevitably become Sutton sympathizers. On 26 August 1870 Henry and William Kelly, sons-in-law of Pitkin Taylor, were arrested on a trivial charge, taken a few miles from home, and mercilessly shot down, while Henry Kelly's terrified wife watched helplessly from hiding. Helm was dismissed from the State Police when his misconduct came to light, but he continued to serve as sheriff of DeWitt County. After Helm's demotion from the State Police, Bill Sutton began to be recognized as the leader of the party.

In the summer of 1872, Sutton sympathizers lured old Pitkin Taylor from his house one night by ringing a cow bell in his corn field and shot him down; he died six months later. During the burial Sutton and his henchmen rode up a nearby knoll, firing their guns and shouting insults. Pitkin's son Jim put his arm around his mother and told her 'Do not weep, mother. I will wash my hands in old Bill Sutton's blood.' His brother Bill and their friends made similar vows.

The first attempt to kill Sutton was made on 1 April 1873, when three of the Taylor clan caught him in a saloon in Cuero, fired through the door, and wounded him. They ambushed him again in June, but he escaped without injury. By now the Taylors had enlisted a major ally to their cause: John Wesley Hardin. A little while later, they waylaid and killed Jim Cox and another member of the Sutton group. Although it is uncertain that Hardin was there when Cox was killed, he was most definitely present when he and Jim Taylor killed Jack Helm in a blacksmith shop in Wilson County.

The very next day after Helm was killed a strong force of Taylors moved on Joe Tumlinson's stronghold near Yorktown. After a brief and inconclusive siege the local sheriff and a posse appeared and miraculously talked both parties into signing a truce; however, the peace lasted only until December, when Wiley Pridgen, a Taylor sympathizer, was killed at Thomaston. Enraged by this murder, the Taylors attacked the Sutton faction, besieged them in Cuero for a day and night, and were besieged in turn when Tumlinson appeared with a larger band of Suttons.

By this time the county was in a state of open war. There were more killings: a man named Johnson in Clinton, another named McVea is Cuero. One John Krohn was also seriously wounded, all in the space of one January week. Bill Sutton finally determined to leave the country, and had boarded a steamer at Indianola on 11 March 1874, when Jim and Bill Taylor rode up to the dock and killed him and his friend Gabriel Slaughter in front of Sutton's pregnant wife.

The Suttons soon got even. Kute Tuggle, Jim White, Scrap Taylor and three others had been engaged to take a herd up the trail for Wes Hardin (who a month or two earlier had killed deputy Webb in Comanche and was now on the run). At Hamilton they were arrested and charged with stealing the cattle, and brought back to Clinton (the three others escaped during a storm). On the night of 20 June 1874, a mob of maybe thirty men took them out of the jail and hanged them. A detachment of Texas Rangers commanded by Captain Leander H. McNelly rode in to restore order; although they tried for several months they were unable to terminate the feud.

On 15 September 1875, after a series of inconclusive trials, Bill Taylor escaped from the Indianola jail during a hurricane in which some three hundred people died; on 17 November Rube Brown, the new leader of the Suttons and marshal of Cuero was shot dead in a saloon by five men generally assumed to have been Taylor sympathisers if not led by Jim himself. Then on 27 December there was a big gunfight in which a gang of nine or ten pro-Sutton men who had not previously been involved ambushed Jim Taylor. He was not yet twenty-four years old.

With Jim Taylor's death the 'old' Sutton–Taylor feud might have come to an end but, just a year later, the Suttons, many of whom were peace officers, were implicated in the murder of Dr Philip Brassell and his son George – who it was said had been involved in the killing of Jim Cox – near Yorktown on the night of 19 September 1876. When the suspected killers laughed at the law, local Judge Henry Clay Pleasants called in the Texas Rangers. For the first time in something like thirty years of feuding, the rule of law was established in DeWitt County. Eight men were arrested at a family wedding and held for trial. After a dozen trials, changes of venue and other legal manoeuvring that went on for more than twenty years only one conviction was ever handed down, and even that person was eventually pardoned.

The Taylor–Sutton feud was over, but there would be plenty more. In fact even as the Suttons and the Taylors were killing each other in Texas, a whole new war was starting up in Lincoln County, New Mexico. This time it was not a feud about land, not about honour or revenge, although both were involved, but about money. This time, out of the gunsmoke would ride a figure destined to become even more legendary than John Wesley Hardin, a frontier drifter who went by the name of Billy the Kid.

THE LINCOLN COUNTY WAR

The so-called Lincoln County War was in fact one of a series of outbreaks of what the military commanders of the day referred to as 'civil disturbances,' a series of 'wars' that ran almost consecutively from the early 1870s to about 1883. The first of these, in 1872, might have been called the Horsethief War, in which incoming American settlers (many of whom would figure in the later conflict) waged war on indigenous Hispanic horse thieves, ambushing or lynching them without compunction.

Hard on the heels of those killings, a 'war' broke out between the Horrell brothers, a tough clan of Texans who had taken a leave of absence from Lampasas County when the law there got too hot for them, and the local native New Mexican population – 'greasers' who were, to a Texan, hardly higher in the evolutionary scale than pond life. The Horrell War raged uncontrollably for almost a year, replete with assassinations, ambushes and even a bloody attack upon a wedding in which three men were killed and two others seriously wounded. When things got too hot even for them the Horrells fled back to Texas, killing and being killed as they went. A year or two later they would become embroiled in another blood feud in Lampasas which ended with brothers Mart and Tom Horrell, under indictment for murder, being shot to pieces in one of the most appalling mob executions in Texas history.

Then in 1876 came the 'Pecos War,' sometimes called 'Chisum's War,' because it was waged by Texas traildriver and cattle king John Simpson Chisum, who had brought his herds into the Pecos Valley in the late 1860s and pre-empted an enormous acreage that stretched from Fort Sumner in the north to the Texas border in the south. In the southern extreme of his range, small ranchers began to congregate in a settlement near the Texas line called Seven Rivers, stealing so shamelessly from Chisum's herds that he finally gathered all his cowboys together in a noisy but unsuccessful attempt to drive them out. Resentments fostered in this collision carried over to the Lincoln County War, the smaller men giving their loyalty to the mercantile firm of L. G. Murphy & Co. on the lines of 'My enemy's enemy is my friend.'

Growing out of the patronage of a powerful political clique known as the Santa Fe Ring and the resulting control of contracts to feed the Mescalero Apaches on their reservation at Fort Stanton, near Lincoln, 'The House,' as the Murphy firm was known, had become the dominant economic and political force in Lincoln County. By means of loans and favours both financial and political they also controlled the law, which they did not hesitate to use for their own purposes, running Lincoln County the way they wanted, controlling the local Sheriff, maintaining a buddy-buddy relationship with the military and appropriating by means both fair and foul most of the government money generated by the Mescalero Apache Indian Agency at nearby Fort Stanton. Against these forces Chisum had until 1876 stood alone, unable to stop the small ranchers and the outlaws who were employed by the House from stealing him blind and selling the cattle to Murphy, who in turn sold them to the government at prices Chisum simply could not compete with.

At the end of 1876, however, a young Englishman named John H. Tunstall arrived in Lincoln County and with the aid and encouragement of both Chisum and his attorney, Alexander McSween, established a ranch, a mercantile store and a bank in Lincoln, making it clear that the intention of the triumvirate was to overthrow the domination of the House and take over its monopoly. By the time Tunstall's challenge materialized, the original founders of the House were no longer in charge of its destiny; Lawrence G. Murphy was dying of cancer and his original partner, Emil Fritz, had died while visiting Germany. Murphy's protégé and – some said – adopted son James Dolan took the reins, aided by another Irishman, John Riley.

Many of the small farmers and ranchers in the Lincoln area – especially the Hispanics who had smarted for years under the domination of the House – switched their loyalty to McSween and Tunstall. To begin with Dolan used his connections to manipulate the law so that legal proceedings against Tunstall caused the Englishman constant harrassment, but when he refused to buckle under, a writ of attachment was issued for all his property. The Sheriff, William Brady, sent a posse to Tunstall's ranch to confiscate his property, turning a blind eye to the fact that known outlaws with a grudge against Tunstall went with it. On 18 February 1878, several of these men killed Tunstall and what had up to this point been a bloodless struggle erupted into a shooting war.

When lawyer McSween managed to have warrants issued for the arrest of Tunstall's murderers, Sheriff Brady not only refused to recognize them, but arrested the men (one of them young Billy Bonney, known at this juncture as 'the Kid') deputized to serve them. Supporters of the McSween-Tunstall faction read this (correctly) to mean the law would not help them and dubbing themselves 'Regulators,' banded together to effect their own brand of justice.

Two weeks after Tunstall's death two of the men suspected of having killed him were executed by the Regulators; a neutral who tried to intervene was also shot down mercilessly. On 1 April, Sheriff William Brady and his deputy George Hindman were assassinated on the street in Lincoln and three days later, in a gunfight at a sawmill near present-day Ruidoso, the Regulators killed a Dolan supporter variously known as Bill Williams and Andrew Roberts, but not before he blew the top off the head of the leader of the party, rancher Dick Brewer, and severely wounded two others.

Lincoln County became a war zone as armed bands of Dolan and McSween sympathizers hunted each other, occasionally colliding in shooting skirmishes. Then in July 1878 the feud literally came to a blazing climax with the 'five day battle' in the town of Lincoln, when the Dolan faction laid siege to the McSween house in which the Regulators were forted up. After four days of inconclusive fighting in which at least two men were killed, troops from nearby Fort Stanton were marched into town ostensibly 'to protect women and children.' In fact their commanding officer, Lieutenant-Colonel N.A.M. Dudley, supported the Dolan side and stood by without interceding as they set fire to the McSween house and after nightfall killed four men – one of them McSween – as the occupants fled the building.

One of the survivors was young William Bonney, mostly called 'the Kid.' He had worked for Tunstall and played a prominent rôle in every gunfight that had taken place. He now became the leader of what was left of the Regulators, staying alive as best they could in the anarchic lawlessness which followed what the Dolan side called 'the Big Killing.' But at long last intervention by the US government resulted in the dismissal of the pro-Dolan Governor of New Mexico Samuel Axtell. He was replaced by Civil War General Lew. Wallace who instituted a campaign of military-style warfare against the outlaws who were terrorizing Lincoln County.

His policies seemed to work but just when it looked as if the war was over, it appeared to flare again in February, 1879 when lawyer Huston Chapman was murdered in Lincoln by a drunken gang. Lew. Wallace met secretly with the Kid, who had been with the gang, and promised him a pardon if he would turn state's evidence against the men who had murdered the lawyer, one of whom was Jimmy Dolan. The Kid kept his word and Dolan was indicted for murder. But when the pro-Dolan district attorney refused to honour Wallace's deal the Kid, who was under indictment for the murder of Brady, decided to take no chances and went on the run.

Without any money and no chance of regular work the Kid and his pals turned to rustling cattle and horses, and in the next year and a half became such a plague that the leading citizens of Lincoln County persuaded former buffalo hunter Pat Garrett to run for Sheriff, his sole brief to put an end to the career of the Kid. In December, 1880 – just a month after his election – a posse led by

Garrett killed two of the Kid's closest pals and captured him and three other outlaws. The Kid was imprisoned at Santa Fe for three months awaiting trial, during which time he wrote repeatedly to Governor Wallace seeking his help; Wallace ignored his pleas.

On 9 April 1881, Billy the Kid was found guilty of the murder of Sheriff William Brady and sentenced to death by hanging. He was taken to Lincoln and held in the old Murphy-Dolan store, now the County Courthouse where, on 28 April just fifteen days before he was due to be hanged, he killed the two deputies who were guarding him, commandeered a horse, and rode insouciantly out of town. Seventy-seven days later, around midnight of 14 July Pat Garrett and two deputies were waiting for him when he came into Fort Sumner to see his sweetheart, and one of Garrett's two shots ended the young outlaw's life on the spot.

BILLY THE KID

Billy the Kid's brief life was little more to history than a candle in the wind, yet in spite of the fact that most of what is known about him happened during his final three years on earth, millions of words have been written about it. The date and place of his birth, who his father was, where he lived as a child, all these are still a mystery, and much of what is known about him is fatally flawed by myth.

It can, however, be fairly confidently stated that his real name was probably Henry McCarty, that he lived briefly in Wichita in the early 1870s, that his mother, Catherine McCarty, married a peripatetic mining prospector named William Antrim in Santa Fe in 1873 prior to moving to Silver City where she died eighteen months later.

Henry – Henry Antrim as he was known – turned delinquent following his mother's death and was jailed for petty larceny, escaped from the Silver City jail and turned horse-thief in Arizona. After he killed a bullying blacksmith named Frank Cahill in a deadfall on the fringes of Fort Grant. In the Fall of 1877 he drifted over the line into New Mexico's Lincoln County and signed on as a cowboy for English rancher John Tunstall.

By this time the Kid (he would not be called Billy the Kid until the end of the last full year of his life) had adopted the name – where he got it from, no one knows – of William H. Bonney. Over the course of the following six months he metamorphosed from drifting nobody to undisputed leader of the Tunstall–McSween faction, participating in a series of escalatingly bloody shootouts that included the assassination of Sheriff William Brady and one of his deputies, a gunfight at Blazer's Mill near Lincoln in which two men died and two others were seriously wounded, and ending with the famous 'Five Day Battle' in Lincoln from 14–19 July 1878 which climaxed with the burning of Alexander McSween's house and the death of the lawyer and four others.

For almost a year, in spite of his shameless rustling activities and several further killings, the Kid seems to have kept hoping for amnesty, but Governor Lew Wallace withdrew his promise to pardon him. In November, 1880, John Chisum 'the cattle king of New Mexico' and Roswell mover and shaker J. C. Lea backed the election of Pat Garrett as Sheriff of Lincoln County, his principal – virtually only – task to capture and/or kill the Kid.

Aided by a rag-tag collection of cowboys from the Panhandle who had been sent to lend him a hand, Garrett killed two of the Kid's partners in crime Tom O'Folliard and Charley Bowdre, and captured the Kid himself just before Christmas, 1880.

The Kid was held in jail in Santa Fe for several months and then taken to Mesilla for trial. He was found guilty of the murder of Brady and sentenced to be hanged at Lincoln, scene of the killing, on 13 May 1881. On 28 April fifteen days before the date set for his execution, he escaped, killing the two deputies guarding him in what

had been the old L. G. Murphy & Co. store at Lincoln and rode free –
some say singing.

This time, however, Sheriff Pat Garrett sent out no posses to
round up the fugitive, but waited patiently until word came to him
that the Kid had not done what everyone expected him to do – flee
south of the border into Old Mexico, where no American law could
touch him – but was hiding out near Fort Sumner, about 150 miles
northeast of Lincoln. Taking along two trusted deputies, John Poe
and 'Kip' McKinney, as backup, Garrett sneaked into the old Fort,
whose mainly Hispanic population was, he knew, either sympathetic toward or terrified of the Kid. The one person he could rely on
for help there was rancher Peter Maxwell, whose sister Paulita was
the Kid's sweetheart – a relationship Maxwell wanted terminated.
At around midnight on 14 July 1881, Pat Garrett killed, perhaps even
ambushed the Kid in Maxwell's bedroom.

It was little more than a month or so short of four years since
Billy had killed blacksmith 'Windy' Cahill in Arizona and hit the
outlaw trail. He was probably no more than twenty years old when
Garrett shot him dead: a brief life to give birth to such an enduring
legend!

THE GRAHAM–TEWKSBURY FEUD

Just five years after Pat Garrett's midnight bullet brought the career
of Billy the Kid to its violent end, the Graham–Tewksbury feud
erupted in a remote mountain area called Pleasant Valley north of
Globe, Arizona. No feud in the history of the West has been bloodier,
more ruthless or more tragic. What started it, why it generated such
intensity of hatred and revenge, no one can clearly say: most of the
leading participants died in the feud and as a result were never able
to set down for the record what actually happened. Indeed, to this
day, there are aspects of the Pleasant Valley war that outsiders are

not encouraged to inquire about. It might be said to have been fought over who should have control of the range, sheepmen or cattlemen; but like all feuds it was also about jealousy, hatred, pride and revenge.

All the early settlers in Pleasant Valley were cattlemen, men who had survived stern testing by the Apaches to establish their ranches on this high mountain plateau. To the valley in the late 1870s came James Dunning Tewksbury, a fifty-something Bostonian with a quartet of sons by a now-dead Shoshone Indian mother. In November 1879 Tewksbury married Lydia Ann Shultes, herself twice widowed, who had three children of her own and soon after set up house in a cabin on Cherry Creek, planted peach trees and rose bushes and should, by all accounts, have lived happily ever after.

But in 1882, the same year young John Tewksbury married Lydia's daughter Mary Ann, Iowa-born ex-miner John Graham arrived in Globe, looking to get started in the cattle business. There he met Edwin Tewksbury, who invited him to come look at Pleasant Valley. Before the year was out, John Graham and his brother Tom had driven their cattle into the valley and staked out a stretch of land further up Cherry Creek from their new friends.

It was said the Tewksburys and the Grahams, who worked as cowhands, were not averse to a little mavericking, and one January day in 1883 absentee cattle baron Jim Stinson's foreman, John Gilleland rode over to the Tewksbury place accompanied by his sixteen year-old nephew and a Hispanic, Epitacio 'Potash' Ruiz, to look over the cattle in their corrals (one version) or to go hunting nearby (version two) and rode into trouble. As well as the four Tewksbury boys, both Tom and John Graham boys were there. Somehow, at some dangerous juncture, hard words were spoken and shooting started. Gilleland was killed on the spot by Ed Tewksbury and young Elisha Gilleland was seriously wounded as he and Ruiz fled the scene. Throughout, the Grahams and Tewksburys presented a united front; the charges against them were dismissed.

Somehow, things went bad between the two clans – perhaps Jim Stinson had a hand in that. Anyway, at some point the Graham boys double-crossed the Tewksburys by registering the cattle branded in their name alone. To make matters even worse, the Grahams then swore affidavits accusing the Tewksburys of rustling; soon after the court case ended with the Grahams being arrested for perjury, John Tewksbury and three others got into a gunfight at the Stinson ranch in which John and another man were wounded. To cover their backs, as it were, the Grahams formed an alliance with Jim Stinson and teamed up with the five sons of another new arrival, cattleman Martin Blevins.

Feeling increasingly persecuted, the Tewksburys withdrew into their own circle. Cherry Creek now became a demarcation line: Grahams to the west of it, Tewksburys to the east. In the fall of 1886, perhaps for spite as well as profit, they leased some of their land to prominent northern Arizona sheep raisers and for the first time herds of sheep were driven into what had been exclusively cattle range. The reaction was predictably volatile, and word soon went round that a certain cattle baron was offering $500 for the head of any man who brought sheep south of the deadline. Then in February, 1887 a sheepherder was murdered; there were ghoulish tales that his head had been cut off to prevent identification.

By summer the sheep were gone; but although the cattlemen had won the hand, the game was anything but over. In July, Mart Blevins disappeared; he was never seen or heard from again and his fate remains a mystery to this day. On 10 August Hampton Blevins and a quintet of riders from the Aztec Land & Cattle Company (the Hash Knife ranch) got into a fight at the Middleton ranch with Jim Tewksbury and some others. Hamp Blevins and John Paine, allegedly a gunman hired by the Grahams, were killed. A further attempt to ambush Jim resulted in another Graham sympathizer being shot dead.

On 17 August Billy Graham, the baby of the family, was murdered by Jim Houck, a deputy sheriff and Tewksbury partisan. On 2 September 1887, Tom Graham retaliated with a raid on the Tewksbury ranch in which Bill Jacobs and John Tewksbury were caught in the open and killed. The rest of the clan forted up in the ranch and stood them off; when the half-wild hogs began rooting at the bodies of her husband and his friend, John's wife Mary Ann begged Tom Graham to let her bury the bodies but he refused, saying 'No, the hogs have got to eat them.' The siege continued for three days until a Sheriff's posse arrived and dispersed the attackers.

Two days later at Holbrook, about 75 miles away, newly elected Apache County Sheriff Commodore Perry Owens (named for a noted Civil War naval commander) attempted to serve a warrant for horse theft on Andy 'Cooper' Blevins, who had been boasting around town that it had been he who killed Tewksbury and Jacobs. In the fight that followed – the most noted gunfight in Arizona frontier history – Owens killed Andy Blevins, his sixteen year-old brother Sam and their brother-in-law Mose Roberts and wounded John Blevins.

Now Sheriff William Mulvenon of neighbouring Yavapai County decided that the only way to end the feud was to arrest the leaders of both factions. When he tried to do so at Perkins' store on 21 September 1887, John Graham and Charlie Blevins resisted arrest and were killed; the seven men found at the Tewksbury ranch – including the remaining two brothers – surrendered without a fight. They were indicted for murder and jailed, but at their trial in June, 1888, no one could be found who would testify against them and they were released. The following December, Jim Tewksbury died of tuberculosis. With only Ed Tewksbury to represent that faction and only one Graham (Tom) and one Blevins brother still upright on the other side, it appeared the feud might be at an end; Graham even moved out of the valley to avoid further trouble. Trouble came anyway: in September 1891 George Newton, the only cattleman known to have joined the Tewksburys disappeared while en route to his ranch from Globe. It was rumoured he had been ambushed while crossing Salt River but no body was ever found.

Then in June 1892, Tom returned to Pleasant Valley to sell his ranch and move his cattle to a new location. On 2 August he was ambushed and mortally wounded near Tempe by two assassins who before he died he identified as Ed Tewksbury and John Rhodes. Only Tewksbury stood trial; he was found guilty of murder in December, 1893 and sent to prison, serving two years; the charges against him were dismissed on appeal in 1896. Unexpectedly, perhaps, he then became a deputy sheriff in Globe where he died on 4 April 1904. It is an odd grace note with which to end such a bloody tale.

As in all the 'wars' that preceded it, those ten murderous years in Pleasant Valley proved nothing and established nothing. Now, few traces of the West's longest feud remain: a scattering of tombstones few tourists ever visit, the rickety remains of an abandoned cabin where brave men died; nothing more, unless you count the legacy of hatred and suspicion that lingers to the present day.

GOLD, SILVER... AND LEAD

THE LAWMEN AND GUNFIGHTERS who tamed the cattle towns of Kansas or fought in the famous feuds were neither the first nor the only specimens of their kind: there were good men and bad in every corner of the American West. Some of them died enforcing the law, others – many others – went down defiantly breaking it. In a land so vast, so sparsely settled it was inevitable there would always be bandits and outlaws, men to whom robbery and murder was a way of life, men who knew how to disappear into the trackless wilderness and live off the country.

There were badmen in Revolutionary times. Early in the nineteenth century murderous thieves preyed on travellers using the Natchez Trace – The Devil's Backbone, as they called it – that ran through wilderness of the Mississippi valley from Nashville to Natchez. Among them were highwayman Joseph Thompson Hare, who came up the Trace from New Orleans; the murderous Masons, father and son; the Harpe brothers, Wiley and Micajah, and later John A. Murrell. Murrell, the son of a preacher man, a horse thief, slave stealer, robber and killer, like the Harpes, disposed of his victims' bodies by filling their abdominal cavities with stones and sinking them in rivers.

Black Bart, the gentleman highwayman and Po8 (poet). Bart was in the habit of composing poems and leaving them at the scenes of his stagecoach holdups.

Sometimes the law triumphed against men like these; sometimes it did not; sometimes to make up for the law's inability to deal with the criminals, frustrated citizens took the law into their own hands. To counter outlawry – or, sometimes, to rebel against too much or unpopular law – so-called Regulator or Moderator organizations sprang up during the 1840s, the most notable being those which occurred in Shelby County in eastern Texas (1840–44) when some eighteen men were ambushed or murdered and dozens more wounded or crippled for life, fostering feuds that would endure for another fifty years. Other hotbeds of vigilantism flourished in southwestern Missouri (1842–44) and southern Illinois (1846–50).

In sections of the Texas frontier where courts and jails had not been established, or where officials and juries could not be depended upon, committees of vigilance were often formed to stamp out lawlessness and rid communities of desperadoes. Sometimes these secret bodies degenerated into mob rule or were used for private vengeance, but usually they were made up of law-abiding, responsible citizens who operated against murderers, horse thieves, cattle rustlers, and those who held up stagecoaches and trains.

One of the best known vigilance committees of the many in Texas was the one formed at lawless, godless Fort Griffin, then standing not only athwart the cattle trails north but also the centre of the buffalo-hunting trade. On the night of 9 April 1876, this group, which called itself the 'Tin Hats,' caught a man in the act of stealing a horse and promptly hanged him, leaving a pick and shovel for anyone who cared to bury him. Over the following three months the Tin Hats shot two horse thieves and hanged six others. Two years later, in a spine-chilling execution, they shot to pieces John Larn, a former Shackelford County sheriff who had turned to cattle rustling.

In equally lawless, equally godless gold-rush California, where one of the easiest ways to make money was to murder a man who had just struck gold and take over his claim, vigilante justice came early. In January, 1849 three robbers were tried by a miner's court and hanged at a gold camp called Dry Diggings which thereafter became known as Hangtown (and later when it had lived down its reputation, Placerville). In San Francisco rampant lawlessness was countered by a 'Committee of Vigilance' which hanged four men in 1851, and a further four in 1856, by which time practically every settlement worth the name had a committee of its own. In the year 1855, there were forty-seven lynchings in the State of California.

One of the most notorious examples of lynch law is the myth-ridden story of the vigilantes of Montana. In the rough and ready climate of a mining town or an isolated settlement, it was all too easy for the demarcation lines between law enforcement and summary justice to become blurred: sometimes it seemed as if citizens would tolerate lawlessness to a certain point – but no further. When that point was reached, otherwise law-abiding men would step around or outside legal nicety and pursue summary justice, sometimes based on hard evidence, others on no more than hearsay. Which it was in the case of Henry Plummer, Sheriff of Bannack City in what would become Montana, history has still to decide.

HANGING THE SHERIFF

A heady mixture of managed truth and near-fact permeates the story of Henry Plummer. It goes something like this: a respected law officer and politician (and also ladies' man) over a ten year period in Nevada City, California, during which time he also killed a man named John Vedder and served time in prison for the crime, Henry Plummer (actually Plumer) was jailed again in October, 1861, this time for having killed William Riley in a fracas at a brothel.

Escaping custody, he went to Carson City, Nevada, and from there left for Washington Territory, according to legend taking along a woman who had deserted her husband and three children to go with him. From Washington they moved on to Lewiston, Idaho Territory, where Plummer is alleged to have linked up with local hardcases Cyrus Skinner, Clubfoot George Lane and others who would feature importantly later in Plummer's story.

While ostensibly working as a gambler, the legend continues, Plummer was actually organizing bandit gangs who raided mining camps, robbing and killing miners at will. In 1862 when the Idaho vigilantes began to take an interest in his activities he abandoned his mistress and moved on to gold-rush boom-town Bannack City, then in a part of Idaho that later became Montana. (In fact, Plummer appears to have spent not two years but less than two months in Lewiston, all of which time was devoted to pursuing mining claims. From there he went to Fort Benton, where he met a man named James Vail, whose sister-in-law Elizabeth became Plummer's wife).

The couple moved to Bannack City, but the marriage appears to have been unsuccessful and soon they were living apart. Handsome, intelligent, and well-presented, Plummer soon became popular with the locals. Of course they had no idea he was the mastermind behind a close-knit gang called 'The Innocents' who were responsible for the epidemic of robberies and murders that were spreading terror throughout the area.

Fearing that after a falling-out, his old ally Jack Cleveland would reveal his murderous background, Plummer shot Cleveland in a saloon fight. The wounded man was nursed prior to his death by Bannack Sheriff Henry Crawford, and Plummer became convinced Cleveland had told the Sheriff about Plummer's outlaw connections. Very shortly they had a gunfight in which Crawford wounded Plummer; realizing he was now a marked man, Crawford quit

Bannack, leaving the field wide open for Plummer, who was elected Sheriff 24 May 1863. The following September the miners of Alder Gulch elected him Sheriff of Virginia City as well.

Meanwhile crime increased rapidly: within a few months (again according to legend) something like a hundred miners were murdered or mysteriously disappeared. Late in 1863, led by Wilbur Fisk Sanders, Paris Pfouts and James Williams, the settlers of Bannack and Virginia City formed what would become one of the most notable vigilance committees in American history.

They set to work with a literal vengeance. The first bandit, well-known local badman George Ives, was hanged at Nevada City on 23 December 1863. Just before he died, Ives named another man, Alex Carter, as an accomplice. Right after Christmas a party of twenty-four men rode out to arrest Carter, only to find he had fled after receiving a warning letter from Erastus (Red) Yeager.

There and then the vigilantes elected to hang Yeager and also George Brown (whose crime seems to have been that he actually wrote the letter). At this juncture Yeager fell apart and told them the identities of many of the murderous gang that called itself The Innocents and named Plummer as their leader. They hanged him anyway.

Six days later, on Sunday, 10 January 1864 the committee formed itself into three squads, each made up of perhaps twenty-five men and, surprising Plummer at the Bannack home of his sister-in-law, arrested him. The other two squads rounded up his deputies Buck Stinson and Ned Ray, marched the three of them to the gallows Plummer had himself erected and without ceremony or benefit of trial, hanged them all.

Next, although he had never been implicated in any of the robberies, it was decided to arrest Joe 'The Greaser' Pizanthia 'to see precisely how his record stood in the Terrritory,' as Dimsdale put it.

When Pizanthia refused to surrender the vigilantes attacked the cabin in which he was holed up. The first man into the house got a bullet in the leg, the man behind him was killed. In the orgy of violence that followed a small cannon was dragged to the scene and the cabin was shelled until it collapsed. Only half alive, Pizanthia was dragged out and hanged from a nearby pole, where he was riddled with more than a hundred bullets.

Next to be strung up was Dutch John Wagner, hanged in the same room that held the still unburied bodies of Plummer and Stinson. Back at Virginia City on 14 January the committee decreed that five more of the gang be hanged: Boone Helm, Haze Lyons, Jack Gallagher, Frank Parish and Plummer's old friend Clubfoot George Lane. A week later, nine more 'Innocents' had been lynched, among them Plummer's cronies Billy Bunton and Cyrus Skinner. Not one of them ever had the chance to plead to either court or jury that he was innocent until proven guilty.

The problem with the story of the vigilantes of Montana is that while there is no doubt at all about the number of men they hanged, the case against their victims has been shown to be largely bunk, propagated by Thomas J. Dimsdale, an Englishman whose 'correct and impartial narrative of the chase, trial, capture and execution of Henry Plummer's road agent band' appeared as a series of articles in 1865 and a year later became the first book ever published in Montana. Based entirely and unquestioningly upon what the vigilantes had chosen to tell him, notable among them the multiple 'executioner' X. Biedler, Dimsdale's account of Henry Plummer's life and times firmly cemented a series of untruths and legends into the historical record.

It is a relatively easy matter to establish that during Plummer's fourteen months in the region only eleven robberies and twenty deaths associated with robbery can be documented. It was a fact of mining life that men were more often robbed by their friends or partners than by highwaymen, and such robberies as did take place in the area were by and large badly planned and bungled. Likewise, a good argument can be made that no such outlaw band as 'The Innocents' ever existed and that even the name was a figment of Dimsdale's imagination. Indeed it is doubtful if, for all their murderous ruthlessness, the vigilantes of Montana achieved anything at all, for by 1865, bandits and road agents were again active in the area between Virginia City and Salt Lake where they held up and killed all but one passenger on a Wells Fargo stagecoach.

In fact, banditry continued to flourish, not just in Montana but also in California, which also had its outlaw gangs. In 1852 California Rangers led by Captain Harry Love ran down and killed the notorious Joaquin Murrieta, his henchman Bernardino Garcia, alias Three Fingered Jack, and two others. On 27 January 1857 James Burton, Sheriff of Los Angeles, was ambushed and murdered along with three of his posse by a gang led by Juan Flores and Pancho Daniel. Following a huge manhunt, two suspected gang members were shot, eleven more lynched and one legally hanged. In May, 1858, following an attack on the Rancho San Juan Capistrano by the Jack Powers–Pio Linares gang in which two ranchmen were killed and a woman raped, a vigilance committee tracked down the culprits, lynching seven and killing Linares. Powers escaped only by fleeing into Mexico.

California was notable in that so many of its bandits were of Hispanic origin, perhaps propelled towards crime by the disappearance of the comfortable old rancho system and the ever-growing influx of white settlers who considered them worthless and contemptuously refused to employ 'greasers' for anything other than menial tasks. Working as herders or labourers, banding together when opportunity or inclination presented itself, they were joined by criminals released from San Quentin, desperadoes on their way to or coming from San Francisco, and criminals from the Monterey peninsula or inland San Jose looking for easier pickings. Among the most cunning and violent of these was Tiburcio Vasquez.

Born in Monterey in 1835, Vasquez was still in his teens when he got mixed up with Anastasio García, a vicious outlaw. In 1854 Garcia, Vasquez and another man named José Higuera got into a fight at a dance with a man named William Hardmount, a town constable, killing him. An angry mob of whites lynched Higuera, but Vasquez and García escaped, although the latter was captured and lynched a few years later. That same year, Vasquez was convicted of horse theft and sent to San Quentin prison for five years. As soon as he got out he reassembled his old gang and commenced robbing stagecoaches, rustling and other criminal activities, revelling in his role of bandido. He wore expensive clothes and a large gold watch and chain, always riding the finest horses that could be bought or stolen. He was a ladies' man who loved music and dancing and writing poems to the many inamoratas he seduced and then abandoned.

THE HUNTING OF TIBURCIO VASQUEZ

On 4 June 1870, Tiburcio Vasquez walked free once again from the confines of San Quentin and within a few more months had returned to his old haunts in Monterey County. In the spring of 1871 he teamed up with bandit compañeros, Juan Soto, Procopio Bustamante, Bartolo Sepulveda and others, making their headquarters in an adobe in the isolated Saucelito Valley not far from present-day Los Banos.

Unknown to them a seven-man posse led by San Jose Sheriff Nick Harris which included Alameda County Sheriff Harry Morse was on the trail of Soto, wanted for a January, 1871 robbery at Scott's Corners in the Sunol Valley (which was on Morse's patch) during which a store clerk had been murdered.

Henry Nicholson Morse (1835–1912) who held the office of Sheriff of Alameda County for seven consecutive terms, fourteen years, was a remarkable lawman by any standards. It was said of him that 'no great crime was ever committed within his jurisdiction whose perpetrator escaped final detection and capture.' As much detective as Western-style lawman, Morse was noted for his relentless pursuit and fearless confrontation of outlaws and badmen, several of whom he had killed in gunfights.

When the posse reconnoitred, they found there were three main buildings in the valley, one owned by Juan and Carmela Lopez, a second owned by the Alvarado family but presently the headquarters of the bandits two miles away, and the third, the Storm ranch, about four miles down the valley. Beside the Lopez house there were two rudimentary buildings called jacales.

A plan was devised: Morse and San Jose policeman Theodore Winchell would go down to the Lopez house and arrest everyone in it to prevent any warning being sent to the bandits. The rest of the posse would ride to the Alvarado adobe and arrest the entire band. When Morse got to the house, however, he found several men and women standing in the main room and three more sitting at a table, one of whom was Juan Soto.

'Manos arriba!' snapped Morse, pulling his gun. Soto just glared at him. Two more times More ordered him to put up his hands and still Soto did not move. Morse handed his handcuffs to Winchell and told him to cuff the prisoner, but although he had a shotgun, Winchell was too scared to move. 'Then cover him while I do it!' Morse shouted, but instead Winchell turned and ran. At the same moment a well-built woman grabbed Morse's gun arm and one of the men grabbed the other.

'No tire in la casa!' they yelled, 'Don't shoot in the house!'

As Morse struggled to free himself Soto jumped behind one of the bystanders and began tearing at the buttons on his coat to get at his pistols. Morse got his gun hand free and fired a shot that took off Soto's hat as the bandit brought his gun up.

Morse ran out of the house followed by Soto, who took a shot at him that missed when Morse dropped to the ground. Three more times Soto fired, and three more times – incredibly – Morse ducked the bullets, returning Soto's fire as he retreated toward his horse and rifle. His last shot smashed into Soto's gun, jamming it and Soto ran back to the house. As he passed, Theodore Winchell, standing nearby, fired at him with the shotgun but missed.

As Morse slid his 1866 Henry carbine out of the saddle holster Sheriff Nick Harris came barrelling down the slope on his horse, jumped off and ran to Morse's side, rifle in hand. The two men ran from the house toward a horse tethered to a nearby oak, but the horse, spooked by the gunfire, broke away, and Soto veered right toward another tethered horse.

Morse levelled the Henry and at a range of about 150 yards, shot Soto in the shoulder; badly hurt, the bandit turned and ran at the two lawmen, trying to get close enough to use his sixguns. He never made it. Morse's second shot tore off the top of his head, killing him instantly.

The posse searched all the adobes in the valley, but found only an escaped Santa Cruz jailbird named Gonzales, who told them Busta-mante and Vasquez had gone, and that the man in the blue overcoat had been Bartolo Sepulveda.

On 5 August 1871 Vasquez – who had split up with Bustamante after a quarrel over a woman – held up merchant Tom McMahon between Salinas and San Juan Bautista. A few days later, with the assistance of two accomplices, he robbed a stagecoach near Soap (now San Felipe) Lake. On 10 September although posses from three counties were out hunting him, Vasquez and two other men –

probably Pancho Barcenas and Pancho Galindo – shot up a Santa Cruz brothel and wounded a policeman who tried to intervene. He in turn shot Vasquez through the body and his followers hustled him away. As soon as he was able to travel, he disappeared into Mexico for three months.

Meanwhile Procopio Bustamante was living it up in the brothels of San Francisco's Morton Street, an area so dangerous the police seldom ventured into. Inevitably, he was seen and word was flashed by telegraph to Morse in Alameda. Carrying an arrest warrant – for the theft of a cow! – he and his deputy Lew Morehouse hurried to the city and joined forces with city detectives Appleton Stone and Ben Bohen, who had Bustamante under surveillance in Morton Street.

In the afternoon of 10 February 1872 Morse slipped around the back of the brothel while the other three made a show of entering at the front. As he heard the commotion Bustamante got up to leave, his hand on his gun, but Morse was already behind him. He grabbed the bandit by the throat and jammed the muzzle of a cocked sixgun into Bustamante's ear.

'Put up your hands, Procopio,' Morse told him. 'You're my man!'

Bustamante was tried, convicted and sent to San Quentin for seven years – nothing like the punishment his crimes merited, but the best that could be done. As a result Procopio was back on the street by 1877 and immediately returned to his life of crime. In November of that year he and five others robbed a store in Grangeville and wounded a clerk, and a month later raided the town of Caliente in Kern County, robbing the express office, train depot, hotel and store. Four of the bandits were captured and lynched, but Bustamante wasn't finished yet. On 26 December he and his gang held up a store in Hanford. A posse tracked him down and surrounded the jacal in which he was hiding, but Procopio shot his way out, killing one of the possemen. After that he confined his activities to Mexico, where he is said to have been killed about 1890.

If the misfortunes of his former friends bothered him, Tiburcio Vasquez gave little sign of it. In April, 1872 he had robbed a stage-coach near Hollister, and on 26 February 1873 raided Firebaugh's Ferry, robbing the store and an incoming stage. On 30 July he pulled another robbery near Gilroy, and on 26 August in the village of Tres Pinos he and his gang killed three innocent bystanders while robbing the store and hotel. On 10 November he struck again and on 26 December with ten men backing him up, he took over Kingston in Fresno County, cleaning out the town's two stores and hotel and robbing over thirty citizens of a total $2500.

With a price of $8000 (alive) or $5000 (dead) on his head, Vasquez was hunted by a series of posses, one of them headed by Harry Morse, but the outlaw had too many friends among the Hispanic population who hid him and fed him and lied to the lawmen. As if thumbing his nose at the officers, Vasquez made an abortive raid on a ranch near Los Angeles; when Los Angeles Sheriff William Rowland's posse came after him he not only eluded it but stopped to rob four men during the pursuit.

On 27 April Morse and his men arrived at Fort Tejon. They had been in the field from sunup to sundown for six weeks and were no nearer catching Vasquez now than when they started. Morse was preparing to return north when he got word that Vasquez was holed up in what is now West Hollywood, but when he got word to Rowland, the Sheriff feigned disbelief. Soon after Morse left to pursue other leads, Rowland sent a posse to the cabin Morse had told him about and captured Vasquez, who was brought down by a blast of buckshot as he tried to escape from a rear window.

Tiburcio Vasquez was tried for murder at San Jose in January, 1875 and hanged on 19 March 1875.

Before he gave up chasing bandits, however, Harry Morse would add one more feather to his well-feathered cap, the pursuit and capture of one of the most endearing rogues in frontier history, the Poet Laureate of the stagecoach hold-up who called himself 'Black Bart.'

BLACK BART – OUTLAW AND POET

On 26 July 1875, the stagecoach plying between Copperopolis and Milton in central California was stopped in a lonely spot by a man brandishing a shotgun. Wearing a long linen duster coat, his head covered with a flour sack with cut-out eyeholes and a bowler hat, the bandit politely requested the driver, John Shine, to throw down the strongbox. As Shine reached down, the highwayman shouted 'If he dares to shoot, give him a solid volley, boys!' Looking around, Shine saw what appeared to be rifle barrels pointing at him from the surrounding bushes. Taking no chance, he tossed down the strongbox; when a frightened woman threw out her purse the bandit refused it, saying he wanted only the Wells Fargo shipment. Told to drive the coach a short distance, Shine waited until the robber vanished into the woods, then went back to get the plundered express box. He found the 'rifle barrels' were nothing more than sticks rigged to suggest a well-armed band of thieves.

This robbery – which netted him only $160 – was the first of some twenty-eight hold-ups (some sources put the figure even higher) carried out over the next eight years by the same softly-spoken, courteous man. At the scene of one robbery near Fort Ross in August, 1877 he left the following poem:

> *I've labored long and hard for bread*
> *For honor and for riches*
> *But on my corns too long you've tread*
> *You fine-haired sons of bitches.*

The note was signed 'Black Bart the Po-8' and by that name the humorous highwayman became widely known, the most idiosyncratic and untypical of all Western highwaymen in that he always committed his robberies and departed on foot (it would later be learned he was afraid of horses) and never once, throughout all the years he plied his criminal trade, fired a shot.

A year passed before he reappeared, intercepting the Quincy-Oroville stagecoach on 25 July 1878 and getting away with $379 from the Wells, Fargo box. Once again, he left a scrawled piece of doggerel:

> *Here I lay me down to sleep*
> *To wait the coming morrow*
> *Perhaps success perhaps defeat*
> *And everlasting sorrow*
> *Let come what may I'll try it on*
> *My condition cant be worse*
> *and if there's money in that Box*
> *'Tis munny in my purse.*

Although Wells Fargo offered substantial rewards, it seemed Black Bart had a charmed life. He pulled four robberies in 1878 (two of them on successive days), three the following year and four the year after that, always choosing coaches with no shotgun guard, always near the top of a steep rise where the horses had slowed to a walk. There was no pattern to his strikes, which ranged from Yreka near the Oregon border to the mining country south of Sacramento. He had a narrow escape in 1882 when he tried to hold up a stage en route to Marysville carrying $18,000 in bullion, only to be frightened off by a near miss from the shotgun guard's gun that nearly put an end to his career.

Then on 3 November 1883, when he again stopped the Copperopolis stagecoach at the same spot as his first robbery, Black Bart was wounded by one of the passengers and fled. When Calaveras County Sheriff Ben Thorn and Wells, Fargo detective John Thacker arrived on the scene, they found the bandit had left behind his hat, three pairs of cuffs, an opera glass case and a handkerchief with a distinctive laundry mark 'F. X. O. 7.' Wells Fargo and Harry Morse – who had always believed the bandit was from the San Francisco area – began a systematic search of the laundries in the city, finally locating 'the identical mark' at a Bush Street agency, which also furnished the name of the owner, Charles E. Bolton, a mining man who had rooms on Second Street. Just two hours later, while Morse was still there, Bolton came into the laundry 'elegantly dressed and ... sauntering along carrying a little cane. He wore a natty little derby hat, a diamond pin, a large diamond ring on his finger, and a heavy gold watch and chain,' Morse wrote.

After introductions were made, Morse tricked Bolton into accompanying him to the Wells Fargo office, where he and Jim Hume questioned Bolton for three hours 'until great drops of perspiration stood out on his forehead and nose,' but could not break him down. At about eight that evening, Bolton was taken to his rooming house where they found letters written in a hand which matched the poems left at the robberies. He finally admitted his guilt, cut a deal with the detectives and led them into the mountains where he had concealed about $4000 in a hollow log; on 17 November 1883 48-year-old Bolton pleaded guilty in a San Andreas court and was sentenced to a very lenient six years in San Quentin prison. It transpired that he had been using the proceeds of his stagecoach holdups to pose as a well-off mining man and live it up in San Francisco buying pools on horse races and speculating in mining stocks.

His real name, it transpired, was Charles E. Bowles (Boles) born in Norfolk, England around 1829, one of seven sons and three daughters of John and Maria Bowles. The family had emigrated to the United States a year after Charles's birth and settled in Jefferson County, New York State. When he was about twenty Charles and his brothers David and James joined the gold rush, returning east after two years. In 1854 he married Mary Johnson and settled in Decatur, Illinois. Joining the Army in 1862 he served at Vicksburg, Chattanooga and Atlanta and was mustered out two years later with the rank of lieutenant. He and his family (there were three daughters) moved to Oregon, Illinois where, following the birth of a son, Arian, in 1865 Boles joined the Montana gold rush. He never went back.

What he did in the missing decade between his leaving home and his debut as a bandit remains a mystery, as does what happened to him after he was pardoned in January 1888. It is possible Bolton may have committed three stage holdups before he dropped completely and forever out of sight, and that Wells Fargo offered him a pension of $200 a month if he would leave their vehicles alone. The company of course denied this, but the legend persists. Another story has it that after his release he returned east to marry a childhood sweetheart and died in New York in 1917. Whatever the truth, Bolton disappeared forever. It is one of history's ironies that his name became something of a legend in California, whereas that of Harry Morse, the man who rid California of so many of its badmen, has largely been forgotten.

TOMBSTONE

Not so the name of Wyatt Earp, who around the same time Morse was chasing bandits in California, was dispensing a different sort of law and order in Tombstone, Arizona. He arrived there with his brothers Morgan and Virgil and their wives at the end of 1879, leaving behind him a good, if somewhat speckled, record of police work in cowtowns like Wichita and Dodge City. Tombstone, in the San Pedro valley near the Arizona-Mexico border, had mushroomed into being in 1877 when prospector Ed Schieffelin discovered rich silver outcroppings and founded the Tombstone Mining District. Two years later when the Earps arrived it was still 'a hodgepodge of shacks, adobes and tents' and maybe a thousand inhabitants. Within a year the population doubled and by 1881 had multiplied by ten, making Tombstone as wide open a mining town as any that ever blotted the landscape of the American West.

To begin with Wyatt, who had expressed himself 'tired of lawin',' worked as a security guard for Wells Fargo, then quit to become deputy Sheriff for the Tombstone district of Pima County with Morgan taking over his old job. At the same time he and his brothers began staking mining claims and buying small properties, making serious efforts to establish themselves, financially and politically, as responsible businessmen. When Cochise County was formed on 1 February 1881 with Tombstone as county seat, Wyatt ran for Sheriff but was defeated by John Behan. He acquired an interest in the gambling tables at the Oriental Saloon and encouraged Dodge City cronies like Bat Masterson and Luke Short to work them. In June his brother Virgil was appointed chief of police and in October Morgan was appointed special officer.

The Earps were consolidating their position and might even have succeeded had it not been for the enmity they generated among the 'cowboy' element, personified by local ranchers like N. H. 'Old Man' Clanton and his three sons, Ike, Phin and Billy plus a hard crew of hangers-on – some did not hesitate to call them rustlers – that included the McLaury brothers, Frank and Tom, Johnny Ringo, Curly Bill Brocius and others. This gun-hung gang liked the Earps not at all and were not afraid to use their weapons to defend or assert any of their rights they felt the Earps might trample on.

In March 1881 the two factions became sworn enemies after a stagecoach was attacked near Contention and driver Eli 'Bud' Philpot and another man were killed. Wells Fargo's agent Marshall Williams assembled a posse that included Wyatt, Morgan and Virgil, Bat Masterson and others and set out to find the holdup men. Next morning they were joined by Sheriff Johnnie Behan, his deputy Billy Breakenridge, and local tough Buckskin Frank Leslie. Three days later they arrested Luther King, who confessed to having been one of the holdup men and named three others as his confederates. King was taken to Tombstone and jailed; a couple of weeks later he escaped and disappeared.

Annoyed at losing an opportunity to boost his chances in the coming election for Sheriff, Wyatt Earp cut a deal with Ike Clanton: if Ike would betray the three stage robbers King had named, he would settle for the publicity of having arrested Bud Philpot's killers and turn the Wells Fargo reward money over to Ike. The deal fell apart when two of the bandits were killed in New Mexico. Then in July, Wyatt's friend, consumptive dentist-gambler John Henry 'Doc' Holliday fell out with his common-law wife, who swore an affidavit that Doc had been in on the robbery, and he was arrested. Although the charges were dropped, the incident created suspicion that the Earps were involved in illegal activities and not the upright lawmen they professed to be.

The reputation of the Earps was somewhat restored after Virgil stepped in as acting marshal when Tombstone's venal Chief of Police Ben Sippy left town and kept going. Big, tough Virgil enforced the ordinances vigorously and arrested violators without fear or favour– even Wyatt, at one point – and by midsummer the brothers were pretty much in control of what happened inside the city limits. Another stage robbery on 9 September saw Virgil leading one posse and Behan another in pursuit of the thieves: Virgil's posse caught up with and arrested Pete Spence and Frank Stilwell – who happened to be Behan's deputy.

Although the charges were dropped the arrests caused bad blood between the cowboy element and the Earps. Frank McLaury, Ike Clanton, Johnny Ringo and some others told Morgan Earp they would kill him and his brothers if they ever came after them. Tom McLaury told Virgil pretty much the same thing. So when in early October Virgil rearrested Spence and Stilwell and the latter was bound over for trial, the situation became tense. At almost the same time, Marshall Williams let Ike Clanton know he was aware of the deal Ike had made with Wyatt, Ike threatened to make the Earps pay for revealing their secret.

GUNFIGHT AT (NEAR) THE OK CORRAL

On the cold, clear morning of 26 October 1881, the Earps learned a very drunk Ike Clanton was prowling the streets armed and looking for a fight. Wyatt, Virgil and Morgan went looking for him; when Virgil found him he buffaloed Ike, disarmed him and marched him into court, where he was fined $27.50. As Wyatt left the courtroom he encountered Tom McLaury who commenced making threats; Wyatt knocked him senseless with his gun and walked away.

Ike and Tom were joined by Frank McLaury and Billy Clanton. After being repeatedly warned by citizens that the cowboys intended to kill them, Virgil Earp asked Sheriff John Behan to help him 'disarm these parties' but Behan refused on the grounds that if the Earps went after the cowboys there would be a fight. Instead he promised he would persuade the boys to leave town.

About half an hour later, although he did not know for sure how many of them would be waiting, Virgil 'called on Wyatt and Morgan Earp and Doc Holliday to go help me disarm the Clantons and McLaurys.' He handed Holliday his shotgun, telling him to keep it out of sight under his coat and the four men set off up Fourth Street and turned on to Frémont.

Six men were grouped on a vacant lot near the OK Corral, between Fly's boarding house and the cabin of former Mayor William Harwood: Frank and Tom McLaury, Ike and Billy Clanton, John Behan and a youngster known as 'Billy the Kid' Claiborne. As the Earps drew nearer, Behan held up his arms. 'For God's sake don't go down there or they will murder you!' he pleaded. Virgil shook his head. 'I am going down there to disarm them,' he said.

Seeing the Earps approaching, the five cowboys backed further into the 18-foot wide lot, almost in line astern. 'Boys, throw up your hands, I want your guns!' Virgil Earp boomed, and within seconds the shooting started – and was over inside half a minute. When the black smoke drifted away, both McLaurys were dead and Billy Clanton mortally wounded; Morgan and Virgil received minor wounds, and Doc Holliday a nick. Ike Clanton had grappled with Wyatt for a moment before running for cover; Billy Claiborne also fled. Afterward, Sheriff Behan tried to arrest the Earps but Wyatt refused to submit.

The gunfight – contemporary writers called it a 'street fight' – was over but the controversy still rages. Although a justice of the peace declared the Earps had been acting as officers of the law, and later a Cochise County grand jury refused to indict them, many others muttered that the Earps had shot down men who had their hands in the air. The bodies of the three dead men were put on display in an undertaker's window with a sign that said:

MURDERED ON THE STREETS OF TOMBSTONE

Threats were made against the lives of the Earps and others, like Doc Holliday and Mayor John Clum, who supported them. A blood feud had been declared.

On 28 December Virgil Earp was the victim of an assassination attempt; although he survived the shotgun attack, his left arm was rendered useless. When in March, 1882, Morgan was shot to death while playing pool, and a coroner's jury named Pete Spence, Frank Stilwell and others as the killers. Wyatt and Warren Earp, Doc Holliday and two others escorted Virgil and his wife to Tucson to catch a train to California. That same night, 20 March, Frank Stilwell, suspected of shooting Morgan, was found dead in the Tucson rail yard.

Wyatt and Holliday were indicted, but refusing again to submit to arrest, Wyatt left Tombstone for Pete Spence's wood camp with his brother Warren and Doc Holliday. Spence surrendered to Sheriff Behan and two other men involved in the killing of Morgan Earp were arrested. Next day at Spence's camp the Earp party killed Florentino Cruz, a 'half-breed' also suspected of involvement in Morgan's death. It was also reported, although never proven, that Wyatt had also killed Curly Bill Brocius in the Dragoon Mountains.

After the last fight, Wyatt Earp left Arizona for good. He talked of returning to Tombstone to face the charges against him and running for Sheriff, but he never did. He and his brothers would never again be the same powerful unit they had once been. In 1883 he made headlines briefly when he was one of a group of former Kansas lawmen who were called to Dodge City to help out Luke Short, run out of town by his business rival, who just happened to be Mayor.

Apart from famously – and controversially – refereeing the Bob Fitzsimmons–Tom Sharkey fight in 1896, he did nothing significant for the rest of his life. He joined the 1884 Idaho gold rush, opened one saloon in Aspen and another in San Diego and dabbled in investments, occasionally plying his trade as a gambler. He also teamed up again briefly with Virgil to run a saloon in Cripple Creek in 1885 and again in Nevada, where Virgil died, a decade later. Wyatt outlived him by more than twenty years, cashing in his chips on Sunday morning, 13 January 1929, an almost forgotten relic of the old frontier.

But only 'almost.' Fuelled first by books, then movies, and later television, Wyatt Earp – a man who was never more than a deputy sheriff or an assistant marshal – was transformed into the most famous lawman of the frontier West. Controversy still swirls around his name and his life. Was he a saint or a sinner, a rugged frontiersman or a sly opportunist, a pimp and crooked gambler or an incorruptible lawman, a small-time peace officer or a mendacious fabulist?

No matter: thanks to the legend of the gunfight at the OK Corral, his frock-coated legend stands as tall today as that of another Westerner whose life and true character have been lost in a similar mist of myth, that Robin Hood of Missouri who robbed from the rich to give to the poor, Jesse Woodson James.

Quintessential outlaw Jesse James. Betrayed and shot in the back by a colleague, Bob Ford, the legend of Jesse James is perhaps one of the most enduring of the Old West.

CHAPTER SEVEN

BANDITS AND BADMEN

A S THE OLD FOLK SONG about Jesse James says, he was born one day – 5 September 1847 – in the county of Clay, and he came from a solitary race. His parents were Kentuckians, his father Robert James of Logan County an itinerant preacher, his mother Zerelda Cole of Lexington. In 1842, the young couple – Preacher James was just twenty-three and his wife sixteen when they exchanged marriage vows – settled in a simple, three bedroom single storey house on a 275-acre farm in Clay County, Missouri where, on 10 January 1843, they became the parents of a son, whom they named Alexander Franklin. A second son, Robert, died about a month after his birth in 1845. Next came Jesse, and then a daughter, Susan Lavenia, who was born on November 15, 1849. The children never really knew their father, who frequently absented himself from the farm.

In 1850, (driven out, some said, by the sharp tongue of his lanky, forceful wife), Robert James decided to try his luck in the California goldfields. A few months later he was dead, his possessions sold to pay his debts, in a mining camp appropriately called Rough and Ready. Hardships ensued; by April 1851 the family's condition was such that the congregation of the New Hope Church (of which her husband had been pastor) took up a collection for them. With no income, the widow, 'a buxom country lass...and not afraid of the devil himself,' had to find herself a husband. On 30 September 1852, perhaps in haste, she married Benjamin Simms, a 52-year-old farmer. They separated after about nine months; the following January Simms died, possibly after a fall from a horse.

Almost exactly three years after tying the knot with Simms, Zerelda married for a third and final time. The groom was Dr Reuben Samuel, three years her junior, a 'small, meek and quiet man' who did everything in accordance with his new wife's wishes, even to the extent of giving up medicine to run the farm and signing a prenuptial agreement guaranteeing Zerelda ownership of the place and its seven slaves after his death. For all that, it appears to have been an equable arrangement. On 26 December 1858 their daughter Sarah was born, followed by John two years later, Fannie Quantrell in 1863, Archie Peyton in 1865 and Mary in 1868.

By the time Fannie came along Frank (but not Jesse, who remained on the farm) had joined the ranks of Quantrill's Raiders (hence his sister's middle name). William Clarke Quantrill, always known as Charley, was one of the most important of Missouri's guerrilla leaders or 'bushwhackers,' as they were known. In the Kansas-Missouri border warfare raging parallel to the Civil War further east, he had built up a fearsome reputation, leading a band of cut-throats that included George Todd, a desperado of startling ruthlessness. Later in the conflict they joined forces with 'Bloody Bill' Anderson, who for sheer ferocity outdid even Quantrill.

Soon after his induction, Frank took part in an ambush at Richfield (now Missouri City) in which four Federal troops were killed and another seriously wounded. Two nights later the guerrillas raided Plattsburg, capturing weapons and a payroll of about $10,000 before heading for cover near the James-Samuel farm. On 26 May Federal militiamen scouring the country looking for the 'bushwhackers' came looking for Frank. Jesse, who was ploughing a field, was grabbed, beaten, and prodded with sabres but steadfastly denied any knowledge of his brother's whereabouts.

At the house, a Lieutenant Culver was questioning Dr Samuel. When the Doctor professed not to know where his stepson was, the militiamen got a rope and hoisted him up on a tree, whereupon Dr Samuel capitulated and took them to the bushwhackers' camp nearby. A short, sharp engagement ensued in which two of the bushwhackers were killed, but Frank James and his companions eluded the militia and escaped.

The following spring, Jesse – who had been deemed too young the preceding year when he begged them to let him accompany them – also joined the guerrillas, but his career as a partisan came to an abrupt and unheroic halt early in August when he tried to steal a saddle from 54-year-old Ray County farmer George Heisinger, who shot him through the chest. Jesse was taken in a wagon to an inn near Kansas City owned by his uncle, where he was cared for by his first cousin, Zerelda (named after Jesse's mother) 'Zee' Mimms.

He was back in the saddle by September, one of a band of about eighty men under Bloody Bill Anderson who took over the railroad town of Centralia, got roaring drunk after finding a barrel of whiskey, robbed an incoming stage and then at about 11 a.m. stopped a North Missouri Railroad express train carrying 125 passengers and some twenty-five Federal soldiers. The passengers were robbed and the soldiers – apart from a sergeant who for some reason Anderson decided to spare – were executed without mercy. The drunken bushwhackers then set fire to the train (overlooking several thousand dollars in the express car which went up in the flames) and sent it rushing down the tracks with its whistle tied down before abandoning the town.

A detachment of Federal infantrymen arrived at Centralia at

about 4 p.m. Mounted on confiscated horses, and led by Major A. V. E. 'Ave' Johnston, they set off in pursuit of the guerrillas. At the top of a hill overlooking Anderson's camp they dismounted and prepared to fight on foot. The bushwhackers (who outnumbered the soldiers two to one) charged up the hill on horseback like Comanches and in a vicious running fight slaughtered them all – the official count was 125 men, including Major Johnson who, according to Frank James, was killed by Jesse.

On 21 October just a month after the 'Centralia massacre' as it became known, George Todd was killed near Independence and two days later Bloody Bill Anderson's band was ambushed by a detachment of mixed infantry and cavalry near Orrick and cut to pieces. Anderson's corpse was taken to Richmond and photographed. Later his head was cut off and mounted on a telegraph pole, and his headless corpse was dragged through the streets.

The war, particularly in the trans-Mississippi West, was virtually over. On 20 May 1865, Jesse and some other guerrillas were heading for Lexington where they planned to surrender when they ran into a unit of the 3rd Wisconsin Cavalry and in the ensuing skirmish, Jesse was shot in the chest and had to be brought into town in a wagon. Lying in bed wounded at the Virginia Hotel, he took the Oath of Allegiance to the United States and surrendered to the parole. Later, he was once again taken to the Mimms home and cared for by Zee. Soon afterwards they became secretly engaged.

Back home with his family – Frank had also surrendered (he had been with Quantrill in Kentucky on 10 May 1865 when the old bushwhacker had himself been ambushed and mortally wounded) – Jesse recovered from his wound and took stock of the changes war had wrought upon Missouri and upon his own life. To the victors had gone the spoils: they were the law, they had the good jobs, the fat salaries. What did the future hold for young men like himself, tarred with the reputation of having been guerrillas and bush-whackers? The answer was not long in coming.

On Tuesday, 13 February 1866 a group of between ten and thir-teen horsemen wearing Army overcoats rode into Liberty, Missouri and pulled up in front of the Clay County Savings Association Bank. Two men dismounted and went inside, where cashier Greenup Bird (who had once helped administer the estate of Robert James) and his son William sat at adjacent desks. One of them asked for change of a $10 bill, but when William went to the counter he found himself staring into the barrel of a revolver. 'Make a sound and we'll shoot you down,' the man snapped. 'We want all the money in the bank and we want it quick!'

The Birds were then hustled into the vault, which the robbers cleaned out before shutting them inside. Greenup Bird quickly dis-covered they had forgotten to lock the door, threw it open and ran to the window, shouting the alarm just as the robbers mounted up, pulled revolvers, and galloped away, firing as they went; across the street 19-year-old George Wymore folded to the ground, dead. Then they were gone, and with them, over $57,000 worth of currency and bonds.

Whether Frank and Jesse were there is uncertain; at the time their names were not mentioned in connection with the raid, but then, neither of them were known in Liberty. Since Arch Clement was credited as being the leader of the band, it is at least a distinct possibility. At any rate, the first daylight bank robbery ever com-mitted in peacetime in the United States had been successfully carried through; it would be a template for the many more which would follow.

Commencing with (or shortly after) the Liberty raid, Jesse and Frank James soon emerged as leaders of a well-trained and fearless gang of brigands who specialized in armed bank and stagecoach holdups, ranging for sixteen years over half a dozen midwestern States: Iowa, Kansas, Arkansas, Kentucky, Alabama, West Virginia and, of course, Missouri. In the commission of their crimes, something like a dozen citizens were killed and perhaps as many again wounded, not counting their own losses.

Although sometimes the figures involved are approximate, this is a conservative estimate of the sums stolen by the various incarnations of the James gang in bank and stagecoach robberies:

October 1866	*Lexington, Mo.*	*$2000*
March 2, 1867	*Savannah, Mo.*	*NIL*
May 23, 1867	*Richmond, Mo.*	*$3500*
November 27, 1867	*Independence, Mo.*	*$30,000*
March 20, 1868	*Russellville, Ky.*	*$12,000*
December 7, 1869	*Gallatin, Mo.*	*$900*
June 3, 1871	*Corydon, Iowa*	*$6000*
April 29, 1872	*Columbia, Ky.*	*$1000*
July 21, 1873	*Adair, Iowa*	*$2300*
January 15, 1874	*Hot Springs, Ark.*	*$2000*
January 31, 1874	*Gad's Hill, Mo.*	*$3000*
December 8, 1874	*Muncie, Ks.*	*$30,000*
September 6, 1875	*Huntington, WVa.*	*$15,500*
July 6, 1876	*Otterville, Mo.*	*$15,000*
September 7, 1876	*Northfield, Minn.*	*$26*
October 8, 1879	*Glendale, Mo.*	*$6000*
September 3, 1880	*Mammoth Springs, Ky.*	*$1200*
March 11, 1881	*Muscle Shoals, Ala.*	*$5200*
July 15, 1881	*Winston, Mo.*	*$600*
September 7, 1881	*Blue Cut, Mo.*	*$300*

TOTAL (round figures): $136,500
(estimated present-day value: approximately $15,000,000)

BANK ROBBERY AS A PROFESSION

By 1874 Jesse James was no longer an obscure Missouri thief, but a national figure who commanded headlines with every strike he made. During the Gad's Hill robbery, however, the gang had rifled registered mail being carried by The Adams Express Company. Its president William Dinsmore decided to meet this new threat head-on and hired the Pinkerton National Detective Agency – the same agency which had broken up the Reno brothers' train robbing gang – to bring it to an end. Shortly thereafter the US Post Office added its imprimatur to Pinkerton's activities, with what would be deadly effect.

Founded in 1840, the Pinkerton Agency had provided security for President Abraham Lincoln and intelligence-gathering facilities for General George McClellan during the Civil War, activities that led directly to the establishment of the US Secret Service. It was the first truly national organization, free from the usual constraints that hampered county or state law-enforcement officials, dedicated to identifying, tracking and apprehending not only the thief but also his loot.

Pinkerton assigned three detectives to the task of locating the train robbers: Louis Lull and John Boyle were charged with locating the Youngers, J. W. Whicher the James boys. With mind-boggling naïvety Whicher went straight to Kearney and began asking local lawmen questions about the James boys. Appalled by his stupidity they warned him not to go near the place. 'The old woman would kill you even if the boys don't,' they said. He went anyway, posing as a labourer looking for work. Next day his dead body was found at a nearby crossroads with three bullets in temple, neck and shoulder. A note pinned to his jacket said 'This to all detectives.'

Lull and Boyle fared no better. Having enlisted former deputy

Sheriff Edwin Daniels to help them find the Youngers, they had stopped at a farmhouse near Monegaw Springs to ask directions. The three men rode away unaware that Jim and John Younger had been inside the house, guessed they were detectives and decided to follow them. Boyle fled as the Youngers approached; when they caught up a gunfight erupted in which Daniels and Jim Younger were killed and Lull, badly wounded, died three days later. When the news reached him, Pinkerton was appalled and angry. 'There is no use talking,' he said of the bandits, 'they must die.'

On 24 April 1874, just six weeks after the murder of Whicher, Jesse married dark, diminutive Zee Mimms at her sister Lucy's home in Kearney and they left for a honeymoon at Jesse's sister Susan's home in Texas. Later that same year, Frank James eloped with Independence farmer's daughter Annie Ralston and joined them there, no doubt formulating plans to generate some extra income now that they were both married men. When it came, it came in abundance: in a robbery at Muncie, Kansas, on 8 December 1874, Jesse, Frank and the three Younger brothers got away with about $30,000 from the Wells Fargo express box, doubtless to enjoy a very merry Christmas. Although huge rewards were posted – the governor of Kansas offered $2500 each for the robbers, the Kansas Pacific added $5000, Wells Fargo posted a $5000 reward for the return of the stolen property and $1000 for each outlaw dead or alive – nobody seemed anxious to try and collect them.

Meanwhile, one of Pinkerton's spies, Jack Ladd, was working on the farm of Dan Askew, and a US Post Office investigator in Kearney was vetting any mail addressed to the family. It was Pinkerton's intention to mount a raid on the farm as soon as he knew for sure that Jesse and Frank were in it. 'Above all else destroy the house,' he told Samuel Hardwicke, organizer of the raiding party, 'wipe it from the face of the earth.'

On 25 January 1875 Jesse and Frank were seen at the farm. At 11.30 that night, unaware that the brothers had left shortly after nightfall, Hardwicke's men set fire to the weatherboarding on the kitchen side of the farmhouse. Then they battered in one of the boarded-over windows and threw in a special device, a seven-and-a-half-inch diameter iron ball filled with combustible material obtained from the Rock Island arsenal.

Awakened from his sleep by cries of alarm from the slaves sleeping in the kitchen – it was now well after midnight – Dr Samuels pulled off the smouldering weatherboards and quenched the fire. His wife Zerelda went to the kitchen where she saw the iron ball burning on the floor. She tried to kick it over but could not; just then Dr Samuel came in, got a shovel, and pushed the strange object into the fireplace. By now everyone was awake and had come into the kitchen. As they stared at the alien object it exploded, sending huge chunks of cast iron shrapnel whirring in every direction. Dr Samuels and one of the slaves were hit by small chunks of metal. A larger one tore off Zerelda Samuel's right arm just above the wrist and another smashed through 6-year-old Archie Samuels' body, fatally wounding him.

The explosion was heard two or three miles way. The first person on the scene was the Samuels' neighbour, Daniel Askew. Others arrived soon after, doctors were summoned. Zerelda's shattered lower arm was amputated below the elbow – without benefit of anaesthesia – and shortly, Archie died. An inquest was held, and later a grand jury interrogated witnesses; quite soon the involvement of Hardwicke and Askew had become public knowledge. People in Clay County held their breath; no one doubted there would be retribution or that it would be long in coming.

On 12 April Daniel Askew left his house after dark to get some water from the well. Three bullets were pumped into his head as he made the return journey: it was widely understood they had been fired by Frank or Jesse James, more probably both. On hearing the news, Pinkerton's spy Jack Ladd disappeared, and Samuel Hardwicke fled to Minnesota. No one was ever tried for the murder of Archie Samuel. Jesse and Zee moved south to Edgefield, a small town in Tennessee across the river from Nashville where they were known as Dave and Josie Howard. According to his young cousin George Hite, Jr, Jesse went to Chicago and stayed there several months awaiting an opportunity to kill Allan Pinkerton. Mere assassination would not do. 'I want him to know who did it,' he told George. 'It would do me no good if I couldn't tell him about it before he died.' He felt confident, he said, that some day God would deliver the detective into his hands. Instead, on 31 August his wife delivered him a baby son, who was named Jesse Edwards James,

It would appear that although they lived 'normal' lives in between their forays into bank and train robbery, Jesse and Frank James never seriously considered any other way of making a living. Though members of their gang were sometimes caught and punished it must have seemed to the brothers that they had charmed lives. They always seemed to know more about the banks they robbed than most of the citizens in the town. Their timing was always good and their horses always the best that money could buy, a factor that weighed heavily in their ability to evade or outrun pursuit and capture. That is, until they tried to rob the First National Bank of Northfield, Minnesota.

7 September 1876 was an ordinary Thursday. At two o'clock in the afternoon three horsemen – Jesse James, Bob Younger and Charlie Pitts – wearing long white duster coats rode abreast across the iron bridge spanning the Cannon River into Mill Square, Northfield. Across the square and to their right was Division Street, and on the corner the Scriver building housing the First National Bank. Dismounting outside the bank they tied up their horses and sat down on some packing cases. Several minutes later another three riders,

similarly attired, crossed the bridge and halted in the middle of Mill Square. Seeing them arrive the trio outside the bank got up and went inside as two more horsemen – Cole Younger and Clell Miller, wearing identical linen dusters – came up Division Street and dismounted in front of the bank, Miller taking up a position in front of the bank door while Cole Younger pretended to tighten his saddle cinch in the middle of the street.

In a small town like Northfield, where most people used wagons rather than saddle horses, the strangers immediately attracted attention. J. S. Allen, a local man, crossed the street to see what was happening, but when he got close to the bank Clell Miller grabbed him. 'Don't you holler, you sonofabitch!' he growled, but Allen broke free and ran around the corner yelling 'Get your guns, boys – they're robbing the bank!'

As Allen raised the alarm, Cole Younger swung into the saddle and fired his pistol into the air, a signal to the trio in Mill Square, who thundered into Division Street with pistols blazing, joining Cole Younger to ride up and down the street yelling 'Get in, get in!' at people on the street.

Inside the bank the three robbers had jumped over the counter and ordered the assistant cashier, Joseph Heywood, to open the safe. 'There's a time lock on it and it can't be opened,' he lied (in fact, the vault was unlocked, and if the bandits had merely tried the handle they could have opened it). When Charlie Pitts grabbed Heywood and threatened to kill him, Heywood broke loose, shouting 'Murder! Murder! Murder!' at the top of his voice. Pitts fired his gun to frighten the man into silence at almost precisely the same moment as Cole Younger fired his warning shot outside.

As Clell Miller tried to mount his horse, townsman Elias Stacey fired off a shotgun loaded with birdshot which hit Miller in the face. As the outlaw rolled on the ground in pain another citizen, Henry

Wheeler, grabbed an old .52 calibre carbine and headed to a third-floor window in the Dampier Hotel overlooking the street. At the same time hardware store owner A. R. Manning picked up a Remington rolling block rifle and headed for a doorway from which he shot Charlie Pitts' horse, wounded Cole Younger in the hip, and then killed Bill Chadwell with a bullet through the chest. By now the citizens had all armed themselves and the street outside was a hell of flying lead.

'Come out of the bank, for God's sake, they are shooting us all to pieces!' one of the bandits shouted. As the men inside, who had not only failed to open the vault, which contained about $12,000, but also missed several thousand dollars in the teller's drawer, ran for the door, one of them turned and shot Heywood through the head.

Outside, from his eyrie in the Dampier Hotel Henry Wheeler put a bullet through Clell Miller's chest, then as Bob Younger came out of the bank, a shot from Wheeler's rifle smashed his arm. Shifting his pistol to his left hand Bob kept shooting as his brother Cole turned his horse back up the street to pick him up. As Bob swung aboard, Cole was hit almost simultaneously in the shoulder and the side while another bullet ripped away the rear of his saddle.

Prevented by the townspeople from leaving town by the iron bridge, the surviving six outlaws – Jesse and Frank James, Cole, Bob and Jim Younger and Charlie Pitts – galloped south out of Northfield down the Dundas road, leaving behind the dead bodies of Miller and Chadwell and bank cashier Joseph Heywood. Lying mortally wounded in the street was a Swedish immigrant, Nicholas Gustavson, who had been told to get out of the way and didn't move fast enough.

The bandits were in bad shape: with the telegraph flashing word of their probable whereabouts ahead of them, a 1,000-man posse (the biggest in US history) was forming. The only man in the gang who could have guided them safely back to Missouri, Bill Chadwell, was lying dead on the street in Northfield. They had no food and were a horse short. The loss of blood from Bob Younger's smashed arm made him so weak that even though he was riding double with Cole, he had trouble staying in the saddle and passed out more than once. His brother Jim had a bullet in his shoulder: Cole himself, hit once in the hip, also had buckshot wounds in the shoulder and side and possibly other flesh wounds. Frank James had a bullet wound in his thigh. To add to their misery, it began raining heavily, relentlessly, and did not stop for two weeks.

After they were nearly taken by a posse at Minneopa Falls near Mankato (by which time their horses had given out and they were on foot) they decided to split up, Frank and Jesse going one way, the Youngers and Pitts the other. On 21 September, two weeks after the Northfield debacle, Charlie Pitts was killed and the Younger brothers captured in a boggy wood by a rag-tag 'posse' near Madelia – about twenty miles south of New Ulm, scene of the Little Crow uprising. Shot to pieces, the prisoners were taken to Madelia. When a woman sympathized with him, Cole Younger shrugged. 'We're rough men,' he said, 'and we're used to rough ways.'

By pleading guilty to all the charges against them the Youngers avoided hanging and were given life sentences. Bob died in 1889, but Jim and Cole were pardoned and paroled in 1901. Jim committed suicide the following year, but Cole lived on until 1916. When he died he still had sixteen bullets in his body. In 1991 the gun he used at Northfield was sold at auction for $211,500.

And what of Jesse and Frank? For a month there were hundreds of reports of sightings of them in Minnesota, Iowa, the Dakotas and Nebraska, their desperate journey headline news all over America.

Somehow, stealing horses, posing as possemen, cattle buyers, even fishermen, they made their way southwest to the Mississippi valley and finally home. Badly shaken by the events at Northfield, they moved south to Tennessee and for the next three years 'went straight,' Jesse using his old alias Dave Howard, and Frank calling himself Ben J. Woodson. But Jesse could not afford to go on living the life of a prosperous merchant and racegoer indefinitely and in 1879, with another mouth to feed – a daughter, Mary, was born on 17 July 1879 – he formed a new gang and although Frank would have nothing to do with it, went back on the outlaw trail.

But time was running out for Jesse James. Improved communications, the universal use of the telegraph and another new-fangled invention, the telephone, were making crime more difficult and pursuit and capture more likely. There would be only four more robberies (one of them the last robbery to take place on the old Natchez Trace), none of them yielding large amounts of cash. Living with his family in a bungalow in St Joseph, Missouri, under the name 'Thomas Howard' Jesse was planning to rob a bank in Platte City with two of his newer recruits, Bob and Charlie Ford. Unknown to him, the brothers had met with Missouri Governor Thomas J. Crittenden and Henry Timberlake, Sheriff of Clay County who promised them ten thousand dollars apiece for Jesse and Frank James, dead or alive. So when Jesse took off his guns – something he hardly ever did – and got up on a chair to dust a picture on the wall, Bob Ford seized the moment and shot him in the back of the head.

Six months later, Frank James surrendered to Governor Crittenden, stood trial, and was eventually cleared of all the charges against him. In later years he teamed up with Cole Younger in an (unsuccessful) Wild West show and died at the old James farm near Kearney in 1915. Long before his death, myth had begun to overtake the truth about himself and his brother and Jesse James had become an American legend.

THE DALTON GANG

But if Jesse was gone, there were plenty of others ready, willing and able to take his place. In the Midwest, the inheritors of the James and Younger brothers' legacy were the Dalton brothers who, amazingly – or on reflection, perhaps not so amazingly – were cousins of the Youngers and kin of the Jameses. Grattan Dalton, born in 1861, Robert (1867), and Emmett (1871) were three of the fifteen children of horse trader, stock raiser and saloonkeeper James Lewis Dalton and Adeline Younger.

Lewis, as he was known, was 36 when he married 16-year-old Adeline Younger at Independence, Missouri. During the Civil War the family moved west from Cass County, Missouri (where Grat, Bob and Emmett were born) and settled in Montgomery County, Kansas, then in 1882, when the boys were in their teens, to Indian Territory. In 1884 an older brother, Frank, became one of a hard-riding cadre of US deputy marshals at Fort Smith, Arkansas, celebrated in the old adage 'No Sunday west of St Louis, no God west of Fort Smith' and for its 'hanging judge,' Isaac Parker, a stern and tireless guardian of the law.

He needed to be. In the wilderness west of Fort Smith the Indian Territory crawled with horsethieves, cattle rustlers, bootleggers, thieves and murderers of every colour and stripe. During the two decades Judge Parker held office he tried over thirteen thousand cases, sentencing 160 men to hang; seventy-nine of whom were actually executed, some sixty expertly dropped to their doom by Parker's ace hangman, George Maledon. In the same two decades, sixty-five marshals died in the line of duty, fifteen of them inside two years, one of whom was Frank Dalton, killed on 27 November

1887 while attempting to arrest horse thieves with another officer. His place was taken by his brother Grat, unofficially assisted by Bob and Emmett; their wages were the only income the family had, for, after moving back to the Coffeyville area in Kansas, shiftless, foot-loose Lewis and his wife had separated.

In 1890 Lewis died and Adeline moved back into the Indian Territory, settling at Kingfisher, not far from Oklahoma City. By now, the Dalton brothers, with Bob at their head as chief of the Indian police in the Osage Nation, were moonlighting as rustlers and horse thieves and selling 'protection' to whisky runners. Pretty soon they quit law enforcement and their part-time thievery became a full time profession. Bob, although not the eldest, was the leader. Tall, blond, blue-eyed, he was a ladies' man, an expert horseman and a dead shot who killed a man named Charles Montgomery in 1889, some say for horse theft, others say over a woman. Grat was also tall, blond, and blue-eyed and like Bob, quick to fight, but a heavy drinker and not very bright. Emmett, the baby of the trio, was a gentler, dreamier fellow. With the Daltons rode Bill Powers and Bill Dalton, both of whom had worked as cowboys with Emmett. Other occasional companions were 'Black-faced Charlie' Bryant, so called because of a black powder burn on his face, 'Bitter Creek' George Newcomb, Charley Pierce and Dick Broadwell.

After a short sojourn in New Mexico, the boys rode west to Tulare County, California where their brother Bill was a state assemblyman. In February 1891 the brothers were accused of robbing a Southern Pacific train at a wide spot in the road called Alila. Bob and Emmett skinned out with a $1500 reward on their heads and headed back to Indian Territory. Grat and Bill were arrested and tried; Bill was acquitted but Grat was sentenced to imprisonment. According to legend – which is probably all it is – he escaped from the train taking him to the penitentiary by making a daring dive into the San Joaquin River, returned to Indian Territory and rejoined the gang. Bill also returned to Kingfisher, where he set up and succeeded in the land-dealing business, also acting as a spy for his brothers.

On 9 May 1891 the Dalton gang robbed a Santa Fe train near Perry, Oklahoma, and another on 15 September at Leliaetta; on 1 June 1892 they hijacked a train near Red Rock, getting away with about $3000. Their next target was a train at Adair, where they got away with about $17,000. Unknown to the robbers there were eight guards on board and a gunfight erupted as they fled with their loot. As they left town they fired indiscriminately at men on a store porch, killing one and severely wounding another.

Murder warrants were issued at Fort Smith and the railroad put up a reward of $5000 a head for the capture of the gang. This was the biggest bounty ever posted for a single gang of outlaws and with every man's hand turned against them the Daltons began to think about getting out of the Territory. First, however, they needed money. Bob came up with the idea of robbing not one but two banks simultaneously in Coffeyville, Kansas. Bill Doolin, Charley Pierce and Bitter Creek George were either dropped or backed out; Bob, Grat, Emmett, Broadwell and Powers elected to go ahead.

THE COFFEYVILLE RAID

On 5 October 1892, the five outlaws rode towards Coffeyville. It was a beautiful bright clear autumn day. The preceding night they had flipped a coin to see who would attack which bank. They were in high spirits. Bob had tied his coat collar up with a kerchief and Emmett told him 'Just wait till we get to Coffeyville. You won't need any coat, brother. It's going to be hotter than hell up there.' Little did he know.

The raid began to fall apart even before it began. Like the James gang at Northfield, the bandits had made no reconnaissance. They

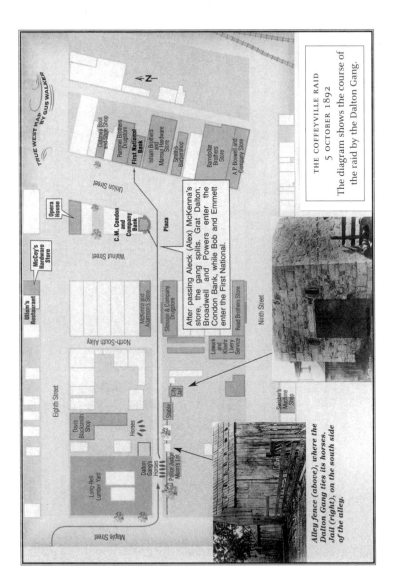

TRUE WEST MAP BY GUS WALKER

Long-Bell Lumber Yard

Davis Blacksmith Shop

Dalton Gang's Horses

Police Judge Munn's Lot

Horses

Stable

City Jail

McKenna and Adamson's Store

Slosson & Company Drugstore

Lewark and Kloehr Livery Service

Read Brothers Store

Swisher's Machine Shop

Ninth Street

North-South Alley

Walnut Street

Union Street

Maple Street

Eighth Street

Ulom's Restaurant

McCoy's Hardware Store

Opera House

C. M. Condon and Company Bank

Plaza

Cubine's Boot and Shoe Shop

Rammel Brothers Drugstore

First National Bank

Isham Brothers and Mansel Hardware Store

Smith's Barbershop

Barndollar Brothers Store

A.P. Boswell and Company Store

—>N—<

After passing Aleck (Alex) McKenna's store, the gang splits. Grat Dalton, Broadwell and Powers enter the Condon Bank, while Bob and Emmett enter the First National.

Alley fence (above), where the Dalton Gang ties its horses. Jail (right), on the south side of the alley.

THE COFFEYVILLE RAID
5 OCTOBER 1892
The diagram shows the course of the raid by the Dalton Gang.

had intended to tether their horses to the hitching rail outside a hardware store on a corner next to the bank, but when they got there they discovered the streets were being repaired and the hitching rails had been removed. Instead they rode into an alley behind a blacksmith shop more than a hundred yards from the two banks and tied up there horses there.

As they left the alley and crossed the street towards the Condon Bank on its 'island' between Maple and Union Streets and the First National Bank beyond it on the far side of Union, dry goods merchant Aleck McKenna recognized the Daltons, who he knew well. He watched them go into the Condon Bank, saw the levelled Winchesters, and shouted the alarm. Word flashed around town like wildfire – the Daltons were robbing the bank! Citizens ran towards the Isham Brothers' hardware store two doors down from the First National Bank, or Boswell's further south on Union, where handguns and Winchesters and ammunition were passed to anybody who wanted one. Then they took positions and waited.

Inside Condon's Bank, as Bill Powers and Dick Broadwell guarded the two doors, Grat Dalton tossed a grain sack on to the counter and told two employees to fill it from the cash drawer. Next he turned his attention to the vault, the outer door of which was open. He yelled at cashier Charles Ball to open the inner door. With magnificent aplomb (because he knew the vault was already open and that there was something like $40,000 in there) Ball told him it was on a time lock and would not open until 9.30.

'What time is it now? Grat said.

'Nine twenty,' Ball lied (it was actually 9.40).

Demonstrating either unbelievable self-control or monstrous stupidity, the outlaw said, 'We'll wait.'

But ten long empty minutes are hard on even the strongest nerves and the bandits began to get twitchy. 'God damn you, I think you're lying to me!' Grat Dalton shouted at Ball. Somehow the bank man again placated him. Perhaps he had seen, as the robbers astonishingly had not, that the town's heavily-armed defenders were gathering outside at almost point-blank range, pushing wagons together.

Meanwhile in the First National Bank, Bob and Emmett Dalton had encountered three customers in the bank as well as three bank staff; another customer walked in while Bob was piling money into his grain sack. Emmett kept them all covered while Bob raged at the (deliberately) slow-moving cashier. Settling for what they had – more than $20,000 – Bob and Emmett herded the bank staff and customers into the street ahead of them. As the two bandits emerged, the citizens cut loose. Bob and Emmett skittered back inside the bank, as did two of the bank employees as the people of Coffeyville poured lead into the two bank buildings.

As the windows of the Condon Bank were shattered by bullets, it finally dawned on Grat Dalton that he might be in trouble. As bullets tore through the walls and windows, he asked the bank staff if there was a rear exit. No, they lied. And Grat took their word for it, not even bothering to check. A bullet shattered Dick Broadwell's arm and he dropped his Winchester. Another shot turned Bill Powers half around, mortally wounded, as another citizen fell, shot through the foot.

From the First National Bob Dalton put a bullet through the hand of one man as he handed the grain sack stuffed with money to his brother. Unlike his slow-witted brother across the street, Bob knew the First National had a back door. Herding one of the bank staff in front of them, he and Emmett stepped out into the alley. As they did a young clerk, Lucius Baldwin, came toward them holding a pistol. Bob shot him dead, then he and his brother ran around to Union Street to where they could see the townspeople firing at the Condon

Bank. Bob levelled his Winchester and put three bullets through one of them. Another man ran to pick up the fallen citizen's rifle, and Bob shot him dead, too.

Now Grat Dalton decided to get out as well. Stuffing the currency from the grain sack inside his shirt and abandoning the silver bullion he had planned to appropriate he led the way into the street. Firing as he ran he headed for the alley where the horses were, Broadwell and Powers lurching along behind him as Bob and Emmett gave them covering fire.

Grat Dalton and Bill Powers were both hit as they ran but they kept going. Another shot hit Broadwell and he went down. Powers was next; hit in the back he fell dying beside the horse he had never had a chance to mount. Still firing wildly Grat Dalton stumbled, half dead, down the pitiless alley. At that moment town marshal Charles Connelly ran out into the alley only to turn the wrong way and Grat shot him in the back.

Once again the outlaw tried to get to his horse, but two more citizens, John Kloehr and Carey Seaman were in the alley now. Kloehr's bullet broke Grat's neck. Unbelievably, Dick Broadwell managed to get into the saddle and kicked his horse into a run but before he was out of the alley Kloehr and Seaman hit him, the first with a rifle bullet, the second with a load of buckshot. Reeling in the saddle, Broadwell kept going. Meanwhile, Bob and Emmett had run south from Eighth Street down a narrow alley that ran into the one where the horses were tethered. As they emerged into view the citizens at Isham's hardware store opened up on them. Bob was badly hit and sat down hard on a pile of cobblestones, firing his rifle from the hip as John Kloehr popped up behind a fence. Another shot – maybe Kloehr's, maybe someone else's – hit Bob in the chest and knocked him flat.

Hit twice, once in the body and once in the arm, but still

clutching the grain sack full of money, Emmett Dalton got into the saddle. As he spurred the horse into a run he was hit twice more. Looking back he saw his brother Bob with his back to a wall, and incredibly, in that murderous hail of gunfire, he turned the horse back and tried to pull Bob up into the saddle with him. As he did Carey Seaman stepped out into the open and fired both barrels of his shotgun into Emmett's back.

Somebody shouted 'They're all down!' The firing stopped and citizens came running into the alley from every direction. Emmett Dalton raised the only hand he could move in surrender, and it was all over.

Death Alley – as they called it and still do – was like a charnel house, weapons scattered in the dust, blood everywhere, the dead bodies of five men and the several horses that had been killed in the crossfire. Later Dick Broadwell's body was found about half a mile out of town, his horse standing quietly nearby. In addition to Marshal Connelly, three other citizens had died – bootmaker George Cubine, 46, shoemaker Charley Brown, 59, and preacher's son Lucius Baldwin, 23 – all victims of Bob Dalton's deadly aim. Two others had been seriously wounded. The battle of Coffeyville was over.

In the alley, banker Haz Read picked up the sack containing his bank's money. A group of men dragged the corpses of the four dead bandits together in a row and photographs were taken. Another man collected the fallen weapons as willing hands carried the dying Marshal Connelly and Emmett Dalton over to Slosson's drugstore, where a mob of men burst in, intending to string the outlaw up there and then, but the doctor who was tending Emmett's twenty bullet wounds told them he was going to die anyway.

As it turned out, he didn't. Emmett recovered from his wounds and spent fourteen years in prison before being pardoned in 1907. He settled in Los Angeles, married, and died in 1937. 'The biggest fool on earth,' he said beside his brothers' grave in 1931, 'is the one who thinks he can beat the law, that crime can be made to pay. It never paid and it never will and that was the one big lesson of the Coffeyville raid.'

But there would always be men who believed it would. The bloodstained mantle of the Daltons passed to their one-time partner Bill Doolin (who, according to legend, had ridden with them to Coffeyville that fateful day but pulled out of the robbery at the last moment), Bitter Creek Newcomb and Bill Dalton, Charley Pierce and others. One by one they were wiped out. Bill Dalton fell to lawmen's bullets near Elk, Oklahoma, in 1894. The Doolin gang lasted until 1896, when Doolin was shotgunned to death by lawman Heck Thomas. It was getting tougher and tougher to beat the forces of law and order. But not impossible; no, still not impossible.

US frontierswoman Calamity Jane (Martha Jane Cannery, c. 1852–1903) celebrated for her bravery and her skill in riding and shooting during the gold rush days in Dakota.

CHAPTER EIGHT

THE GENTLER SEX

THERE WERE, OF COURSE, gentler tamers of the West than the prospectors and miners, gunfighters and badmen, soldiers and trailblazers who came like a tidal wave across the wide Missouri in the frontier years. There were also missionaries and priests, determined to bring God to the godless frontier. There were inventors and businessmen, salesmen and painters, wagon-masters and teachers, engineers and newspapermen and actors and tradesmen, few if any of whom ever so much as fired a shot in anger, let alone expected that their names would ever appear in a history book.

Noticeable in many of those same history books is an absence of stories about the women who came with them, who settled the country and brought law, order, peace and prosperity to it. Men might have built the sod-house frontier, but it was women who turned the sod houses into homes. Men might have blazed the wagon trails across the nation, but it was women in the wagons who cooked their food and baked their bread and mended their clothes and made their soap and raised their sons and daughters.

'The chief figure of the American West,' wrote Emerson Hough, 'is not the long-haired, fringed-legging man riding a rawboned pony, but the gaunt and sad-faced woman sitting on the front seat of the wagon, following where her lord might lead, her face hidden in the same ragged sunbonnet which had crossed the Appalachians and the Missouri long before...There was the great romance of all America – the woman in the sunbonnet; and not, after all, the hero with his rifle across his saddle horn.'

But the story of the woman in the sunbonnet was never really written down; such women had no time to keep diaries, even had they been able to find anything except the miserable daily grind of staying alive to write about. So who might it be said best typified the frontier woman? The Shoshoni woman Sacajawea, who led Lewis and Clark across untracked America? Frances Grummond, the shy Tennessee girl who married a soldier and went with him to the wilds of Wyoming, only to have her heart broken when he was killed by Crazy Horse's warriors beside Captain William Fetterman in the hills above Fort Phil Kearny? Perhaps Virginia Reed, of Springfield, Illinois, or Tamsen Donner, from Newburyport, Massachusetts, who were in the wagon train that set out so optimistically from Independence, Missouri for California on that fine spring morning in May, 1846?

Tragic Fannie Keenan, also known as Dora Hand, shot dead in her bed by a drunken cowboy in Dodge City? Rebellious Ann Eliza Young, one of the twenty-seven wives of Mormon patriarch Brigham Young, or Loreta Velasquez, who fought through the Civil War disguised as a man, then went west to catch herself a wealthy husband – and did? Were they 'typical'? Was Josephine Meeker?

THE ORDEAL OF JOSEPHINE MEEKER

In the spring of 1878, former novelist, newspaperman and agrarian reformer Nathan Cook Meeker took over as the new agent at the Ute Indian Reservation at White River, Colorado. With him he brought his wife Arvilla and twenty-year-old daughter, Josephine, a tall, slender, intelligent and assured girl who was a recent graduate from Oberlin College.

Nathan Meeker's mission was to 'enlighten and elevate' the Utes, and he set about it in a for him typically humourless and dictatorial way, determined to make them over in his own image.

'The most serious pursuit of these Indians is horse breeding and racing,' he wrote, 'and only those young men who have no horses will work.'

His solution to this problem was to deprive the Indians of their horses and to set about converting them into farmers.

This the Utes would not have, and it was not long before Meeker's arbitrary and unpopular actions completely alienated them; finally, when one of them quarrelled with him and beat him up, Meeker called in soldiers from Fort Steele in Wyoming to restore order. Although Major Thomas Thornburgh, the officer commanding the column, was anxious to re-establish peaceful relations with them, the Utes read his arrival at the agency as a declaration of war, and on the morning of 29 September 1879, attacked the military camp, killing its commanding officer in the first skirmish.

When news of the battle reached the agency, a dozen or so Utes grabbed rifles and went on a killing spree, shooting down seven white workers, staking Meeker to the ground with an iron tent pole and mutilating his body before burning down all the agency buildings. As they fled Josephine Meeker, her disabled mother and Flora Ellen Price, wife of the post trader, were captured and carried off. Mrs Price begged the Indians not to burn her. 'No burn white squaw, heap like um', one of the Utes grinned.

By the time hostilities ceased following the arrival of cavalry reinforcements on 2 October, twelve soldiers had been killed and another forty-three wounded, while thirty-seven Utes had perished in what they saw as a desperate defence of their tribal lands. On 23

October the three white women were returned. All had repeatedly suffered what Josephine later described as 'outrageous treatment at night' during their three-week captivity. In secret hearings, Mrs. Meeker testified that a Ute named Douglas had raped her; Josephine named Persune, and Mrs. Price identified her assailant as Ahutupuwit, but although everyone 'knew' what had happened, to save the women public embarrassment no public accusation of the Indians was made.

A strange complication arose: when he was arrested and taken into custody Persune claimed he was in love with Josephine and begged her to stay with him as his wife; he offered her all his possessions and was inconsolable when she refused. After peace was restored, the Utes were dispossessed, split up and removed to new reservations. The chief offenders, including Persune, were sent to Leavenworth Prison, as were Douglas and Ahutupuwit.

Later Josephine worked for as while as a copyist in Washington, and as the secretary of a Colorado Senator. She died of a pulmonary illness some years later in Washington DC.

It might seem almost disrespectful to say that Josephine Meeker was lucky, but lucky she certainly was if her fate is compared to that of 14-year-old Olive Ann Oatman, who was captured with her seven-year-old sister Mary Ann near Tucson, Arizona, in 1851 by raiding Apaches who in turn sold the girls to the Mojave Indians. When she was rescued five years later (her sister had died while in captivity), Olive was found 'sitting on the ground, her face covered by her hands, so completely disguised by long exposure to the sun, by paint, tattooing and costume' that her rescuers could not believe she was a white woman. She had completely forgotten English and was considered a mental and physical wreck, yet nevertheless made a remarkable recovery – the word amazing would not be out of place – and later married and had children, living until 1903.

Janette Riker survived a completely different, but no less terrifying ordeal in 1849. Travelling to Oregon late in the year with her father and brother, she remained with the wagon and oxen when the two men went hunting. They did not return at nightfall so she crawled into the wagon to wait out the night, then the following morning set off to follow their tracks to wherever they might lead. She soon lost the trail and had no choice but to return to the camp where she waited for another week, gradually giving up hope. Knowing it would be impossible for her to take the wagon alone through the mountains – it had already snowed higher up – she found an axe and a spade in the wagon and built herself a rude shelter of poles and earth with dried grass jammed into the cracks, stretching the wagon's canvas hood over the top for a roof.

Into this makeshift refuge she lugged the small stove that they had brought with them in the wagon together with a musket, all the blankets and food. There was no meat, so she shot one of the two oxen and butchered it, salting the meat and packing it away as she had so often watched her father do back home. Then she set to work chopping wood for fuel. Winter blizzards closed in, and snow enveloped her shelter from bottom to top; wolves and mountain lions prowled around it at night but fortunately never tried to get in. For three months she came out only to fetch wood and clear the smokehole.

When the spring came, the thawing snow flooded her out and she shifted her things back into the old wagon, living on dry oatmeal and raw salted oxmeat until April when, purely by chance, a band of Indians out hunting chanced upon her location. They were so amazed by her hardihood that they took her to Fort Walla Walla where she was nursed back to complete health. She never did find out what had happened to her father and brother.

Of course, as well as women like Janette Riker who, as the frontiersmen used to put it, cut their own trail and killed their own snakes, there were just as many fly-by-nights and adventuresses who capitalized upon the fact that there were so few women on the frontier that any woman who actually got there could pretty much write her own ticket. 'Women were queens' said one historian, writing about the early days of gold rush San Francisco when there were only fifteen females in the entire city.

In the back country, women-starved miners considered it a privilege just to be able to look at a member of the opposite sex. Westerners who could afford servants found it impossible to keep them. In Fort Abraham Lincoln, maids brought in to clean the officers' quarters were married within weeks of their arrival, leading the US Army to instruct employment agencies to send out only the plainest and least attractive candidates. It made not the slightest difference: within a couple of months even the most positively ugly newcomers had found themselves a suitor. The sad tale of the marital misfortunes of Henry Tompkins Paige Comstock, discoverer of the famous Nevada silver lode which bore his name, wonderfully illustrates the point.

One day Comstock, who was by all accounts several bricks shy of a wagonload, fell madly in love with the wife of a Mormon who arrived at Nevada City in a broken-down old wagon. Although she was plainly dressed in the standard drab calico dress and sun-bonnet, Comstock found her irresistible, and persuaded her to elope with him to Washoe Valley, where a friendly preacher pronounced them man and wife. The bride and groom had scarcely settled themselves in their hotel room when the deserted and hugely indignant Mormon arrived, demanding the return of his partner.

Unfazed, Comstock produced his marriage certificate and defied the Mormon to do likewise. When the man admitted he could not, Comstock made him a counter offer: sixty dollars, a horse and a pistol to settle the whole matter with no hard feelings. Realizing there was little else he could do, the Mormon accepted the deal and left the newlyweds to begin their new life together.

A little while later, Comstock went to San Francisco on business, leaving his wife in the Washoe Valley hotel. At Sacramento he received a telegraph message from a friend informing him that soon after his departure his wife had absconded with 'a seductive youth' from Carson City and that even now the lovers were on their way to Placerville. The outraged Comstock hastened immediately to that town, where he intercepted the runaways and convinced his wife that she was making a bad mistake. Leaving her alone for a few moments he went downstairs; when he came back he found she had skinned out through a window and was on the run again with the lissome lad from Carson City.

Fuming with anger, Comstock hired every horse in the town's livery stables and, promising a reward of $100 to whoever caught them, sent local men riding out in all directions looking for the couple. The following day one of the searchers marched the lovers back into town at gunpoint. This time, Comstock decided to take no chances. Having locked up his wife securely, he told the young man, who had been placed under armed guard, that he was going to see him hanged. Later that night, a new guard came on duty at the jail. As instructed by Comstock, he told the young man that he didn't care to see him hanged for so small a sin, and that he was going outside to take a drink. 'If you're here when I come back,' he said, 'it'll be your own fault.' Needless to say, the young man took the hint and was never seen in those parts again.

As for the young wife, she stayed with her new husband until the following spring, when she ran away with a tall, handsome miner who caught her eye and her fancy. When last heard of, the former Mrs Henry Comstock was working in a beer cellar in Sacramento. If nothing else, it would appear, Western women could be unpredictable. And none perhaps more so than the one they called 'Calamity Jane.'

CALAMITY JANE

Martha Jane Cannery (the surname is spelled any one of half a dozen different ways), known throughout the West as 'Calamity Jane,' is one of the very few women of the West to have had a movie made about her, and a musical at that. There are so many tall tales told about her that it is impossible to separate fact from folklore, yet there she is, smack bang in the middle of one of the biggest legends of all, part of and inseparable from the life and times of Wild Bill Hickok.

She was born, she claimed, at Princeton, Missouri, in 1852. At age twelve she was in Virginia City (Alder Gulch) Montana, and at sixteen she was already consorting with soldiers, and railroad crews building the Union Pacific line near Forts Bridger and Steele, Wyoming. In her highly unreliable autobiography she said she served as a US Army scout between 1870 and 1876, but no official record of any such service exists. She also claimed to have gone to Arizona in this capacity with Custer, but Custer never served in Arizona, although she may have accompanied the 1875 Black Hills expedition.

Her claims to have been an Indian fighter, miner, stagecoach driver, hotel proprietor and bullwhacker (ox team driver) have to be taken with the same large helping of salt. What is more certain is that she was a camp-follower, a vagrant, an alcoholic and a liar. She can be placed at Deadwood in 1876, but her stories that following the killing she cornered Wild Bill Hickok's assassin, Jack McCall, with a meat cleaver are pure fantasy, as was her claim to have been secretly married to Hickok in 1870; however she certainly nursed smallpox victims in the Black Hills area in the late 1870s.

Jane was married on several occasions, but the details are difficult to establish. From one such union, a son was said to have been born in 1882; no further record of his existence has ever been found. Following her (alleged) marriage to Clinton Burke at El Paso in the mid-1880s, there was a daughter, born in 1887, deposited in a convent in 1895 and thereafter lost to history. Jane wandered through the West, frequently drunk, generally rowdy. She made some appearances in a 'dime museum' in Minneapolis in 1896 when her 'autobiography' appeared, and also in the 1901 Pan-American Exposition in Buffalo, New York, where she drove a wagon and team through the streets to advertize her appearance. When she was dismissed after a dispute, she got gloriously drunk and shot up the fairgrounds. Calamity undoubtedly was the name for Jane.

She went back to Terry, North Dakota, 'a broken, sick old woman, worn out at fifty with the hard, careless life she had led', and died there of 'inflammation of the bowels' on 1 August 1903. Crowds lined up to see her body, dressed in white, and a wire fence had to be erected when people began clipping locks from her hair for souvenirs. For reasons that are no longer clear – legend says it was her dying request – she was buried next to Wild Bill Hickok in Deadwood's Mount Moriah cemetery. Described by a contemporary as looking not much better than a busted bale of hay, whatever Calamity Jane was like in life one thing about her is certain: she was no Doris Day.

Nor, for that matter, was John Henry 'Doc' Holliday anything like Victor Mature, Kirk Douglas, Val Kilmer or any of the other movie stars who have played him. Born at Griffin, Georgia in 1851, he was already suffering from tuberculosis when he graduated as a dentist (not a doctor) and practiced briefly near the family home in Valdosta. He drifted west to Dallas, Texas, where he developed a taste for whisky, gambling and trouble. After getting involved in a shooting scrape there, he moved further west to old Fort Griffin, then at the sharp edge of the frontier, and maybe there, or maybe in Wichita, he met the woman who was to be his partner for most of the rest of his short and violent life. Known around the 'sporting house' circuit as Kate Elder, her origins were as unlikely as her eventual fate.

THE SAGA OF BIG NOSED KATE

Time, legend and half a dozen movies have typecast 'Big Nosed' Kate Fisher, or Kate Elder as she was also known, as Doc Holliday's woman, the proverbial dance-hall girl with a gun tucked in her bustle, a flamboyant character who once burned down a hotel in Fort Griffin, Texas to rescue her lover from a lynch mob.

The facts, as always, are somewhat different. Her real name was Mary Katherine Harony, and she was born in Budapest on 7 November 1850. Her father, a doctor, emigrated to the United States in 1862 and settled at Davenport, Iowa. After the death of both parents, a Gustavus Susernihl became the guardian of the two girls. Mary ran away from home – it doesn't take too much imagination to guess why – and by her own account stowed away on a boat going south and assumed the name of Kate Fisher.

Somewhere along the way she married, perhaps to one Simon Melvin, but after the death of her husband and an infant son, headed west. In 1874 calling herself Kate Elder she turned up in Wichita, working in a 'sporting house' owned by James Earp, Wyatt's brother, and the following year worked in Tom Sherman's Dodge City dancehall. She may even have been Wyatt Earp's consort prior to (or even simultaneously with) meeting Doc Holliday, whom she later claimed to have married in 1870 at St Louis (although no record of any such marriage has ever been found).

Once she met Doc they became inseparable. She accompanied him to Las Vegas, New Mexico, in 1879 and they stayed there a year before moving on to Tombstone. She laid convincing claim to having been an eyewitness of the famous 'OK Corral gunfight' of October 1881, even going so far as to suggest Doc Holliday was very upset by his part in it as it was the first time he had ever killed a man – a somewhat fanciful claim since Doc probably had killed half a dozen men by this time.

When Kate gave testimony implicating him in a stagecoach robbery, she and Holliday split up (although she later denied this). After participating in a couple of revenge killings with Wyatt Earp, Holliday went to Colorado and died there on 8 November 1887. Kate dropped out of sight until 1888 when she apparently married one George M. Cummings, but by 1895 they had parted and she was working in a hotel in Cochise, Arizona.

In June 1900 she became housekeeper to John Howard at Dos Cabezas, and remained with him until his death in 1930. In January 1931, using the name Mary K. Cummings, she entered the Arizona Pioneers' Home in Prescott, where she died on 2 November 1940; her true identity remained a secret until many years after her death.

In a profession where a long life was unusual Mary Jane Haroney was something of a rarity, but surely no one would contend she was lucky. And yet she did a whole lot better than her contemporary, Myra Maybelle Shirley, who was born on 5 February 1848, one of the five children of Eliza Hatfield, the third wife of John Shirley and said to be kin of the feuding West Virginia family of the same name, who homesteaded 800 acres of land near Medoc, (later renamed Georgia City) Missouri.

BELLE STARR, 'BANDIT QUEEN'

Comparatively well-educated for a young girl at that time and place, Myra grew up closest to her brother Edwin, known as Bud, who taught her to ride and shoot extremely well. In 1850 John Shirley moved to Carthage, Missouri, where he opened a tavern and livery stable. During the Civil War his son Bud joined the bushwhackers and rode with Jim Lane, drawing his sister Myra into the fray as a courier and spy. When Bud was killed by militia in June, 1864, John Shirley – perhaps sensing what was going to happen (for most of Carthage – including the Shirley hotel – was burned and looted by Union forces) – moved to Sycene, south of Dallas, Texas, where another of his sons, Preston, had a farm.

Some time that same year Jesse and Frank James and four of their fellow bushwhackers hid out briefly at the Shirley place in Texas; Myra is said to have fallen in love with one of them – not Cole Younger as legend would have us believe, but Jim Read, the son of a wealthy farmer who she had known in Carthage. They were married in 1866 (legend has it they were wed on horseback with Bloody Bill Anderson holding the reins, but of course Anderson had been killed two years earlier) and in September, 1868 had a daughter who was christened Rosie Lee but was always called Pearl. Then Jim got mixed up with the Cherokee Tom Starr gang and took a hand in a killing; he and Myra fled to California, where a son James Edwin was born in 1871.

Before long Jim Read was in trouble with the California law and fled once more. Myra took her children back to Sycene where Jim eventually rejoined her, but pretty soon he was in more trouble, charged with rustling, hold-ups and murder. Leaving her children with her parents, Myra accompanied Jim to the relative safety of Indian Territory, where he continued his criminal career until 1874, when a deputy Sheriff named John T. Morris brought it to a fatal end, leaving Myra, to use her own words, 'in a destitute condition.'

Pretty soon she sold the family farm and moved to Galena, Kansas, where she lived with Bruce Younger, a half-brother of Cole Younger's father and the black sheep – which had to be pretty black indeed – of that family, but she was soon involved with Tom Starr's son Sam, a full-blooded Cherokee who was hardly more than half her age. They married in a full tribal ceremony in 1880, by virtue of which Myra Maybelle Shirley Read Starr became by law a ward of the US government. The couple set up home on a 1000-acre farm at Younger's Bend, near Eufaula, Indian Territory on the South Canadian River; from this point on in her life, Myra would be known as Belle (or sometimes Bella) Starr.

The Starr farm soon became a notorious stolen-horse relay station and hangout for outlaws on the run, including the James boys, but Belle and her husband managed to stay out of trouble until 1882, when they were both arrested for horse theft and possession of liquor, a Federal offence in Indian Territory. Belle was sent to the House of Correction in Detroit where she served nine months of her twelve month sentence. When Sam came home from prison three months later they quickly reverted to their earlier bad habits.

Now, however, although she had only one conviction against her, Belle appears to have decided to live up to her reputation, dressing in a black velvet riding dress and a wide brimmed sombrero, with a sixgun strapped around her waist. It was about this time – we must assume Sam was on the run, or perhaps merely complaisant – that Belle became involved with another Cherokee gang leader known as Blue Duck, who specialized in rustling and bank and stagecoach robbery. The romance ended in June, 1884 when Blue Duck was arrested for murder. Arraigned before the court of 'Hanging Judge' Isaac Parker at Fort Smith, he was sentenced to be hanged. The legend that Belle was instrumental in getting that sentence commuted to life imprisonment seems far-fetched.

In 1885 she and Sam offered refuge to John Middleton, a wanted murderer; before long, an intimate relationship had begun between the fugitive and Belle. That ended when law officers flushed Middleton out of hiding and shot him dead as he tried to swim the Poteau River. Sam Starr, also wanted for several robberies, went on the run. Before long newspapers were noising warnings about 'the Starr gang' and in April, 1886, Belle was arrested, accused of having been the leader in a recent robbery and taken to Fort Smith for trial. Although she was found not guilty of all the charges brought against her, Belle's bad luck continued; a short while later her husband shot it out with a law officer at a wedding party. The result was a draw: Sam killed the lawman and the lawman's shot killed Sam.

Belle's response to this calamity was to invite a Cherokee named Bill July, fifteen years her junior, to move in with her. She rechristened him July Starr and he cheerfully fell with her into the profession of horse thieving until, in the early summer of 1887, he was arrested and jailed. To add to Belle's woes her daughter Pearl was pregnant by a married man and her son Eddie was shot while resisting arrest after trying to steal a horse. Belle disciplined him with a whip, beating him so mercilessly that the boy openly hated her and threatened to kill her. To cap it all, she learned that one of her tenants on the farm, Edgar Watson, was wanted in connection with a murder in Florida. In one version of the story, Watson – who had been stealing horses with July and Belle – refused to make a fair division of the spoils and she threatened to expose him. In another, having been threatened by Cherokee officials with banishment from Indian Territory if she ever again harboured criminals, Belle terminated her rental agreement, vilifying Watson and threatening to turn him in.

On Sunday, 3 February 1889 as she was riding home from a court hearing in Fort Smith, Belle Starr was shot dead by an unknown assassin. She was just two days short of her forty-first birthday. Prime suspects included not only Watson, but also Belle's son Eddie and July Starr, said to now be involved with another woman. In the end, no charges were brought against anyone. Belle's death and the manner of it created an almost instant fame: although as far as is known she never killed anyone, nor was she ever the leader of an outlaw gang, her chequered life was perfect fodder for dime novels and magazines like the National Police Gazette which transformed her into 'Belle Starr, the Bandit Queen' directing a wild band of desperadoes with twin sixguns strapped around her middle, ready to rob and kill at the drop of a feathered sombrero. In reality she was a misfit with very unfortunate taste in men who never could make up her mind whether she wanted to be a respectable wife or a flamboyant bad girl.

CATTLE ANNIE AND LITTLE BRITCHES

As must now be obvious from all the foregoing stories, Belle was not by any means the only one to end up on the horns of that particular dilemma. Just a few years after Belle Starr bade the cruel world goodbye, a couple of kids in the Indian Territory fell into exactly the same trap. History knows them as 'Cattle Annie' and 'Little Britches,' the teenage outlaw groupies who in 1893 became hangers-on of the Bill Doolin gang.

Doolin was an ex-cowboy who turned to crime after a shootout in southern Kansas in which two deputies were killed. A cool, dangerous man, he was accused of many crimes including bank and train robbery, selling whisky to the Indians, rustling and even murder, but he was only ever arrested once. He rode with the Daltons on three of their train robbing expeditions before setting up his own gang, which conducted a string of train and bank robberies between October, 1892 and June, 1893. On 1 September 1893 six of the gang were surrounded and attacked by a posse of peace officers at Ingalls and Doolin escaped during the ensuing gun battle – it could easily have gone down in history as the 'gunfight at the OK

Hotel' – in which five or more men died or were mortally wounded.

It was one of this crowd with whom Anna Emmaline McDoulet, fourteen at the time, had become smitten at a local dance, stole a hired man's pants and rode into Ingalls to tryst with her outlaw hero. Later, she introduced her friend Jenny Stevens to another member of the gang. Following the rout of the Doolin band in the September gun battle Annie, now dubbed 'Cattle Annie' by the outlaws, and Jenny, 'Little Britches', were travelling with one Wilson, wanted for rustling and selling whiskey to the Indians.

When deputy US Marshals Bill Tilghman and Steve Burke tracked the girls to a farmhouse near Pawnee, Little Britches made a run for it on horseback. Tilghman pursued her, leaving Burke to arrest Cattle Annie, who was in the house. As she fired shots at him from a Winchester, Tilghman shot Jenny's horse which fell on her, pinning her leg. Although she fought like a wildcat, Tilghman subdued her and brought her back to the farm where he discovered Burke had been having similar trouble with Cattle Annie who he was holding in a bear hug until help arrived.

In August 1895 Judge Andrew Bierer sent both girls to a reformatory in Framington, Massachussetts; when they reached Boston a huge crowd was waiting at the railroad station to see the 'Oklahoma girl bandits'. After a year Jenny was released, but Annie remained in custody until April 1898. Jenny returned to her father's farm at Sinnett, Oklahoma and there is a persistent legend that she later returned east where she worked as a domestic servant and died of consumption in New York while (it is said) engaged in religious work in the slums.

On 13 March 1901 Annie married 21-year-old Earl Frost and settled down near Red Rock. After eight years and two children, they were divorced; it was around this same time Annie joined the '101 Wild West Show'. Later she married W. R. Roach and they lived in Oklahoma City until his death. Annie remained there, as Emma-line Roach, until her own death in 1978. So successful was she at concealing the details of her past that it was not until a few years ago that the details of her later life were finally established.

THE LEGEND OF PEARL HART

At the centre of a story infinitely more intriguing yet less well-known in the annals of the outlaw West than those of Belle Starr or Cattle Annie was a five-foot one-inch Canadian-born blonde who took up the profession of stagecoach robbery in Arizona just as the century turned. Born in 1871, reared by her widowed mother, educated in a girls' boarding school in her home town of Lindsay, Ontario (she said), Pearl Taylor was only seventeen when she met a charming small time gambler, racing tout and sometime bartender who called himself Sam Hart (it probably wasn't his real name) and eloped with him.

According to legend – and most of her story is just that – Pearl Hart eloped from that Ontario boarding school when she was not yet sixteen, but her husband – Sam or Frank (take your pick) Hart – mistreated her and the marriage broke up. Pearl went back home to Mama, but in 1893, following a reconciliation, she accompanied Hart to Chicago where, one version of the story goes, she became enamoured of one of the performers in the Buffalo Bill's Wild West Show.

She left Hart and went to Trinidad, Colorado, where she gave birth to a son, taking jobs as a domestic or hotel maid to support herself. In the end she gave up, sent her son to Ontario to be looked after by her mother, and in 1895 moved to Phoenix, Arizona, where she renewed her relationship with Sam Hart. (In another version, Pearl arrives at Phoenix in 1892 with a tinhorn gambler named Dan Bandman – or maybe that was just another of Sam Hart's aliases.)

Soon a second child, called Pearl, was born, but the relationship was a violent one and broke up when Sam signed up to fight in the Spanish–American War, in 1898. After he disappeared from the picture, Pearl took her baby to Ohio, where her mother was now running a boarding house, and left the child there.

In the spring of 1899, Pearl turned up at a mining camp near Globe, Arizona, got a job as a cook and took up with miner Joe Boot, a former shoemaker and a year Pearl's junior, with whom, on 29 May 1899, she robbed the Globe–Florence stagecoach, netting around $400 from the three passengers on board. It was quickly noted that although the smaller of the two bandits wore male clothing, 'he' was undoubtedly a woman.

Pinal County Sheriff Bill Truman quickly formed a posse and on 4 June Pearl and Boot were captured near Benson. Boot surrendered meekly but the girl fought off her captors, heaping curses on her apathetic partner. She was, Truman told reporters 'a very tiger cat for nerve and for endurance' and would have 'killed me in my tracks could she have got to her pistol.'

The novelty of a female road agent piqued public interest and newspapers played up the story for all it was worth, particularly Cosmopolitan magazine, which seems to have taken Pearl completely at her very unreliable word.

Joe Boot was lodged in a local jail but Pearl was sent to Tucson, where she enlisted the help of another small time crook named Ed Sherwood (or maybe Hogan) to escape – an event which got headline treatment in newspapers as far away as San Francisco. Three months later she was recognized in Deming, New Mexico, by lawman George Scarborough – the same lawman who had shot down John Wesley Hardin's killer John Selman at El Paso just a few years previously – who had seen Pearl's picture in Cosmopolitan.

When he arrested her and her companion in their seedy hotel, she told Scarborough she couldn't go with him because all her clothes were at the laundry. He made her dress in Sherwood's clothes and took her in anyway. He later said she was one of the most foul-mouthed persons he had ever met.

In November 1899 they were tried at Florence, Arizona, Boot being sentenced to thirty years. Amazingly Pearl was found not guilty of the robbery to which she had freely confessed elswhere, but then convicted on a second charge of stealing a revolver and sentenced to five years in the Territorial prison at Yuma, the first woman ever to be sent there. The records for Prisoner #1559 reveal a slightly less classy lady than the tabloid stories wanted their readers to believe, addicted to morphine and of 'intemperate' habits.

Then, one – discredited – story goes, to the embarrassment of all concerned, she almost immediately got pregnant (or managed to convince the management that she had). In fact, Pearl was a model prisoner who kicked her morphine habit, gained weight, even wrote poetry. Most of all she liked to tell her story to the newspapers 'a long-spun tale told in hobo slang and mixed with the philosophy of her kind,' as the Arizona Graphic put it in 1900.

Paroled on 19 December 1902, she got on a train and disappeared. In some stories she toured in vaudeville, in others she appeared in Buffalo Bill's Wild West Show, in still others she went to live with her sister in Kansas City and pursued 'a dissolute life in the city's slums.' The best one of all has it that in 1924 a little old white-haired lady appeared at the Tucson jail and asked if she could look it over. After the chief clerk gave her a conducted tour he asked her why she had wanted to see the calaboose. 'I was in there once', she said. 'I'm Pearl Hart'. Then she hurried away, never to be heard from again.

Some historians believe that after receiving her pardon, Pearl married a man named Calvin Bywater, who had a ranch between

Florence and Globe. She lived quietly and respectably, never revealing her true identity, and died on 30 December 1955. Others aver there is no evidence to factually round out the brief story of the slip of a girl who pulled 'America's last stagecoach robbery'. Perhaps, all things considered, that's exactly as it should be.

CHAPTER NINE

BURY MY HEART AT WOUNDED KNEE

I N 1876 – the year in which the James gang was smashed apart at Northfield and Wild Bill Hickok was assassinated in Deadwood – the Indian Wars reached their high water mark in the most famous of all the thousands of collisions between white men and Indians, the battle of the Little Big Horn, George Armstrong Custer's famous 'last stand.'

The origins of this disastrous defeat lay in an expedition Custer had commanded two years earlier, when he had taken his 7th Cavalry into the Black Hills of Dakota, land promised in perpetuity to the Sioux in the Treaty of 1868. This expedition was to establish whether there was gold in the Black Hills, and indeed there was: 'from the grass roots down,' according to Custer's ebullient report. By the following spring, hundreds of miners were heading into the Sioux lands and the Army did little or nothing to stop them. When the Indians protested, a commission was sent out to 'treat with the Sioux for the relinquishment of the Black Hills,' land which had been only a few years earlier considered worthless, fit only for Indians to live on.

The Sioux haughtily rejected the commissioners' six million dollar offer and the negotiators returned to Washington to report their failure. They recommended that instead of dealing further

A lone US soldier surveys the aftermath of the massacre at 'Wounded Knee' in South Dakota. The dead bodies strewn in the snow all around him are those of the massacred Sioux and Minneconjou Indians.

with the Indians, Congress simply appropriate the land and give the Sioux a sum fixed as 'fair equivalent' of the land's value. In November Ezra T. Watkins, special inspector for the Indian Bureau, reported to Washington that the Plains Indians living outside reservations were well-fed, well-armed, arrogant and independent and therefore a threat to the maintenance of the reservation system. Troops should be sent against the recalcitrants immediately, he recommended, 'the sooner the better, and whip them into subjection'. A month later an edict was issued to all Indians off the reservations that if they did not come in and report to their agencies by 31 January 1876, 'military force would be sent to compel them'.

Even had they wanted to come in, the non-agency leaders could not have done so because blizzards and sub-zero temperatures had closed down the northern plains and made travel impossible. So, on 7 February 1876, when they failed to meet the impossible deadline set for them, Sheridan was instructed to commence operations against the hostile Sioux bands led by Sitting Bull and Crazy Horse. He in turn ordered Generals George Crook and Alfred Terry to prepare for immediate military operations in the Sioux country in Montana watered by the Powder, Tongue, Rosebud and Big Horn Rivers 'where Crazy Horse and his allies frequented.'

It was the command 'immediate' that was unusual: the US Army had only rarely previously marched against the Indians in such inclement weather. Bitter experience had taught its leaders one thing about their foe: 'unless they are caught before early spring,' as Sheridan advised his superiors, 'they can not be caught at all.'

As a result of this early start their arrival in the Sioux heartlands was unexpected On 17 March Crook's advance column under Colonel Joseph J. Reynolds made a surprise attack on a camp led by Two Moon and Little Wolf of the Cheyenne and Low Dog of the Oglala, destroying all the food and saddles and capturing some twelve hundred Indian ponies. In spite of this setback, the warriors counter-attacked, returning after dark to recapture most of their horses as the bluecoats fell back. Angry with Reynolds – who was later court-martialled – Crook returned to Fort Fetterman to recoup.

All hopes of a successful winter campaign dashed, Terry now concluded that it would not be feasible to move against the hostiles until the spring. Even that prognosis would turn out to be optimistic, for it was not until 17 May 1876 that Terry's command marched out of Fort Abraham Lincoln in North Dakota. It was a major expedition, consisting of nearly one thousand men and a supply train of 150 canvas-topped six-mule wagons, with the Gatling gun battery bringing up the rear. On one side of the train was a beef herd, on the other a remuda of replacement horses and mules. As the band played 'Garryowen', two companies of the 17th Infantry and one of the 6th marched together, while well out in the front and rear on both flanks was a three-company battalion of cavalry.

Twelve days later, Crook's column marched north from Fort Fetterman. Neither he nor Terry had an explicit instructions from Sheridan. The job of each, either or both was to find and commence 'chastising the Indians should it have the opportunity.' The problem was – as always – that they had no idea where to look. Despite miserable weather, Custer's column reached the junction of the Yellowstone and Powder Rivers on 7 June. Two days later he was joined by General Terry and Colonel Gibbon on the steamboat Far West and following a scout by Major Reno of the 7th Cavalry learned from the latter that the Indians were not on the Rosebud as had been thought.

With no clear idea of where the enemy might be, Terry's overall attack plan had to be based on an assumption they were probably in the upper Little Big Horn River. His strategy was a simple one: Custer would advance up the Rosebud valley, Crook would come north toward the Rosebud from his base camp on Goose Creek while Terry and Gibbon would make a semi-circular sweep along the Yellowstone and then up the Big Horn River where the whole force would conjoin against the hostiles. Significantly, they had no idea at all how many of them there were.

After the fight on the Powder River the Cheyennes and Oglalas had headed north through the frozen land until three days later they reached Crazy Horse's camp. Crazy Horse now led these people to the mouth of the Tongue River where Sitting Bull and the Hunkpapas had wintered. Still moving northward this large band was joined by others, Brulé, Sans-Arcs, Blackfeet, Sioux and more Cheyennes who had not returned to the reservations, making an encampment of several thousand. As the snows melted and the grass greened, still more warriors who had left the reservation joined them, bringing news that the Bluecoats were coming, Three Stars Crook from the south, He Who Limps (Colonel John Gibbon) from the west, and One Star Terry and Long Hair (Custer) from the east.

On 17 June Crook's column was attacked by about a thousand warriors under the command of Crazy Horse. In the all-day fight * that followed – the Battle of the Rosebud – Crook's force was out-manoeuvred and outfought; after dark he retreated back down the valley to await reinforcements. No word of this engagement reached Terry, so the whereabouts of the Indians remained a mystery to the columns coming south from the Yellowstone.

After their victory on the Rosebud, the Indian leaders led their people to the valley of the Little Big Horn (which they called Greasy Grass) where large herds of antelope had been seen. When the encampment was made it stretched almost three miles along the banks of the river. No one knows for certain how many Indians were there, but it could hardly have been less than ten thousand, of whom perhaps three or four thousand were warriors.

On 22 June the 7th Cavalry passed in review before General Terry, massed trumpets supplying the martial music. Then amid clouds of choking dust beneath a torrid and cloudless sky, the regiment – 31 officers, 566 enlisted men, 35 Indian scouts and maybe a dozen others – began its march up the Rosebud, 12 miles the first day, 33 on the second. On that day, 24 June scouts brought Sitting Bull the news that Long Hair Custer was advancing up the valley. Next morning the soldiers had crossed the ridge between the Rosebud and the Indian encampment and were marching toward it. Realizing the enemy now knew he was coming Custer made his decision: make a reconnaissance in force against the Indian encampment employing the entire command, and let a battle plan take shape as events dictated.

CUSTER'S LAST STAND

Since the day it happened, controversy has shrouded the battle fought by the 7th Cavalry and Indians led by Sitting Bull and Crazy Horse on the banks of the Little Big Horn River on 25 June 1876. Shorn of interpretation and speculation, what is known for certain is that it began when, upon that day, Custer's Indian scouts told him there was a very big village up ahead of the column. He was overjoyed. 'Custer's luck!' he exclaimed. 'We've got them this time!'

As we have already seen, Custer did not believe there were enough Indians in the world to whip the 7th Cavalry. He prepared to attack and, according to fairly standard Indian-fighting procedure (it had worked at Sand Creek, it had worked on the Washita) he divided his command into three battalions, planning to attack the village from three directions. Three companies (A, G and M) set out under the command of Major Marcus A. Reno; three (H, D and K) under Major Frederick Benteen; and five (C, E, F, I and L) under his own command. One final company (B) was left to protect the pack train carrying extra ammunition; this would follow the command as closely as possible.

Benteen and his 125 men were sent to make a scout to the left of the trail; Custer with about 225 took one side of Sundance Creek (later renamed Reno Creek) leading toward the Little Big Horn valley, and Reno leading 140 officers and men took the other. About two miles from the Little Big Horn River they could see some of the Indian camp. Custer ordered Reno to go down into the valley, cross the river and attack, promising him the support of 'the whole outfit.'

He himself swung his column to the right, clearly planning to attack the village at the other end.

By this time it was just after 2 p.m. The last sight Reno and his men had of Custer was on a hill off to their right, waving his hat exuberantly.

Advancing at a trot and then a gallop towards the village, Reno ran head on into a large force of hostiles whose opposition halted the charge and put the cavalry on the defensive. Reno had never fought Indians before; dismounting his men he deployed them correctly in skirmish line, every fourth man holding the horses, fighting on foot, but they were unable to hold back the increasing numbers of Indians coming to attack them. They began retreating as best they could towards a thicket near the river, the Indians swarming all over them, picking off soldiers like flies.

In this hell of noise and death, troopers panicked and ran for their lives as Reno ordered a retreat from the woods to the bluffs on the other side of the river. As he did so the scout Bloody Knife riding alongside him was hit between the eyes by a Sioux bullet, spattering brains and blood in Major Reno's face and so disconcerting him that he ordered his men to dismount and then immediately to remount.

Within that first furious engagement lasting perhaps twenty or thirty minutes Reno had already lost fifty-five of his 112-man command, some missing, most dead. Virtually leaderless, the column struggled across the river, making no effort to rescue their wounded, and taking up positions on the bluffs on the other side.

As the survivors blazed frantically away at the Indians, Benteen and his column came over the bluffs to reinforce them. Although they were still keeping up a heavy fire, for some reason the Indians were not crossing the river to come after them; Benteen had seen none at all. He had however received a message from Custer's adjutant, Lieutenant Cooke: *'Benteen. Come on. Big village. Be quick. Bring packs. P.S. Bring pacs*[sic].*'*

Pinned down by the Indians as they were Benteen could see no way of obeying these instructions. In fact, through the next few hours the embattled cavalarymen constantly wondered why Custer was not coming back to relieve them. But Custer had other problems on his hands.

As planned, he had taken his command over the deceptively rolling hills on the north side of the Little Big Horn in a long, looping march aimed to end at the further end of the Indian village. His tactics had been basically sound, but as at the Washita he had neglected to reconnoitre the ground on which he expected to fight. The terrain he had to cross was channelled and broken with numerous gullies, making progress over the ten miles he had to cover much slower than expected. By the time he reached his position opposite and above the encampment, Reno was already in rout.

When Reno's column had appeared below the encampment, Cheyenne leader Two Moon was watering his horses when he saw 'a great dust rising. It looked like a whirlwind. Soon a Sioux horseman came rushing into camp shouting 'Soldiers come! Plenty white soldiers!" Rallied by Gall of the Hunkpapas, most of whose family had been wiped out by Reno's opening volleys, within minutes nearly all the Indians there had thrown themselves into the attack against Reno, with no apparent thought of danger from any other direction.

'Then I saw the white soldiers fighting in a line,' Two Moon said. 'Indians covered the flat. They began to drive the soldiers all mixed up – Sioux, then soldiers, then more Sioux, and all shooting. The air was full of smoke and dust. I saw the soldiers fall back and drop into the river like buffalo fleeing.'

Now when word reached the men fighting Reno that another force was nearer to the village, they wheeled their ponies and thundered back through the valley to fall upon Custer's column with devastating effect. 'The blood of the people was hot and their hearts bad,' one of them said, 'and they took no prisoners that day.'

Outnumbered perhaps ten or even twenty to one as they faced the Indians coming up at them from the valley, Custer's 225 troopers could only make a fighting retreat to the higher ground behind them. The lines of their retreat can still be seen today in the scatter of stone memorials to the men who died in it. Being able to see what happened does not however give more than an inkling of what frantic on-the-spot decisions were being made as it did.

Perhaps Custer felt if he could reach the higher ground he might be able to hold out until Reno's command broke through, but he never got there. Another wave of Indians led by Crazy Horse swept around the hill and came over it, falling in an irresistible tide on Custer's rear. He fell – with many of his officers and men – on the river side of what is now called Custer Hill.

Although Custer was down, the fight was not yet over by any means. The surviving cavalrymen fought like tigers, perhaps still buoyed by the hope that reinforcements must soon arrive. But they were doomed. The rifles of the enlisted men jammed repeatedly as the breeches overheated from constant firing; the dust was thick and blinding, the fighting hand to hand.

The lines of markers on the present day battlefield clearly tell their own moving story of the retreat as Custer's men fought their way slowly back towards – they hoped – help in the form of Reno's or Benteen's columns. Lieutenant James Calhoun was probably one of the last officers to die, surrounded by a last defiant cluster of men. His marker is a long way from where Custer fell.

The battle – it probably lasted little more than an hour – was over. Dead on the battlefield were Custer, his brothers Tom and Boston, his company commanders Keogh, Yates, Crittenden, Smith and Calhoun, newspaperman Mark Kellogg, Custer's nephew Autie Reed. Miles Keogh and most of I Company fell in the ravine nearby. The rest of the command lay scattered where they had died.

The body of Sergeant James Butler of L Company was found almost half a mile away from the scene of the major action, nineteen shell cases indicating he had sold his life dearly. Did he evade death only to run into another killing zone? Did he crawl there, badly wounded, still wondering where the hell Reno and Benteen were?

They were still dug in on the bluffs above the river. They had heard the sounds of the battle and cheered, confident Custer was thrashing the Indians. As opposition dwindled – the Indians who had been taking potshots at them were drifting off to join in the looting of the bodies on the Custer battlefield – Reno's officers urged him now was the time to saddle up and go to Custer's assistance. But Reno, traumatized by the awful experiences he had undergone, elected to remain where he was.

Finally, Captain Thomas B. Weir reconnoitred towards Custer's position as far as a high point that now bears Weir's name. There, dimly seen in a distant haze of dust, they made out hordes of Indians. Shots were still being fired – probably victorious Indians celebrating, although Weir did not know that – but at this juncture the Indians were seen to be returning, so the troops retreated to the bluffs and dug in, making shallow trenches that offered little or no cover whatsoever.

The full wrath of the Indian fighting force now descended on them, armed now with weapons and ammunition snatched up from Custer's column and occupying higher ground than that sheltering the soldiers. By nightfall, eighteen troopers had been picked off and another forty wounded. The fighting eased as darkness fell, and a courageous detail slipped and slithered its way down to the river to bring much needed water for throats and bodies parched by the heat and dust of the day.

At dawn the Indians attacked again, and their first charge very nearly rolled right over the defenders, but they held grimly on. Shooting went on most of the morning, tailing off towards the middle of the day as down in the valley the hostiles set fire to the grass and then, concealed under a heavy pall of drifting smoke, struck their camp and moved away down the valley.

Unwilling to take the chance the disengagement might be a trick, Reno and his men remained where they were throughout the night. The following morning, 27 June, a large dust cloud was seen in the distance and the weary troopers got ready to fight again. Before long however, they could see that this time it was a military column. Two officers rode down to investigate. Their first questions to each other were identical: 'Where the hell is Custer?'

General Terry sent Colonel Gibbon down to check out the now deserted encampment on the river. One of Gibbon's flanker scouts, Lieutenant James Bradley, chanced upon the naked bodies of the first dead and then the whole ghastly scene unfolded.

The Indians had stripped and mutilated almost every body on the field, amputating arms, legs and heads in victorious frenzy. Many were scalped, a particular form of retribution. Custer was found in a half-sitting position shot through the chest and head; his body had not been mutilated.

The 208 bodies they found in the vicinity of Custer Hill were buried as decently as was possible – equipped for Indian fighting, the command had few shovels with them – but the bodies of several officers were never located. The bodies of two enlisted men were also missing and have been, over the years, the reason for the legend of a survivor of the battle of the Little Big Horn.

But there were no survivors.

The news of the 'Custer massacre' reached the East on Independence Day, as Americans everywhere were celebrating their country's first Centennial. The nation was stunned, and loud were the demands for punitive vengeance on the savages who had perpetrated this unholy outrage. It was not long in coming. On 22 July William Tecumseh Sherman was given complete military control of all reservations in the Sioux country, and authority to treat all Indians upon them as prisoners of war. Less than a month later a law was passed which effectively appropriated the Powder River and Black Hills country on the grounds that by making war against the United States the Indians had violated the treaty of 1868.

Troops in Wyoming and Montana carried out winter campaigns against the Indians, opting for harassment rather than confrontation. The following spring, Sitting Bull led his people across the Canadian border where he hoped to be allowed to live in exile: it was not to be. In May of the same year, on the promise of a reservation for his people in the Powder River country, Crazy Horse surrendered at the Red Cloud agency in Nebraska. The following August rumours circulated that he was planning another outbreak and he was arrested. When soldiers tried to take him to the guardhouse he resisted and was bayonetted to death.

One by one all the other tribes were penned on reservations. Some fought bravely, others went tamely; it made no difference in the end. In 1873, resisting efforts to make them return to the Klamath reservation, a small band of Modoc Indians briefly waged war in the lava beds of northern California. Led by their resourceful chief Kientpoos, whom the white men called Captain Jack, they fought the US Army to a standstill even though sometimes outnumbered twenty-to-one. Following the murder at a peace parley of General E. R. S. Canby and another commissioner, J. E. Thomas, a retaliatory attack scattered the Modocs into small bands which were hunted down one by one. After their – it has to be said inevitable – surrender, Captain Jack and the other leaders of the uprising were tried and hanged. Their warriors decimated, the survivors were rounded up and removed from their homelands.

In 1874 during what became known as the Red River War, Colonel Ranald Slidell McKenzie, who had taken command of the 4th Cavalry four years earlier, stumbled upon a large encampment of Kwahadi Comanches, Kiowas and Cheyennes in Palo Duro Canyon, a vast sheltering chasm in the middle of the Llano Estacado – the Staked Plains of the Texas Panhandle.On 28 September, just before dawn, the soldiers swept through the village, burning tipis and capturing more than a thousand horses as the Indians scattered and fled.

McKenzie added a new dimension to his campaign strategy. He knew that without horses the Comanche would be helpless, unable to hunt, unable to seek shelter as winter drew in. Without hesitation he ordered the slaughter of all but a few hundred ponies he gave to his own scouts. Within weeks, small groups of Indians began surrendering; soon all were on the reservation except the Kwahadi war leader Quanah and perhaps four hundred warriors. McKenzie sent them an ultimatum: surrender or be destroyed. On 2 June 1875 they appeared at the Fort Sill reservation and the reign of the Comanches was over. The ringleaders were imprisoned at Fort Marion in Florida

In 1877, the year Queen Victoria was proclaimed Empress of India and Rutherford B. Hayes became President of the United States, the government – which had only two years earlier promised them the

Wallowa valley in Washington state forever – ordered the non-treaty Nez Percé tribe to move on to a reservation in Idaho. The officer sent to arrange this expeditiously was General Oliver Otis Howard, famous for having made peace with Cochise and the Apaches four years earlier. When the Nez Percé leader Joseph and his lieutenants White Bird, Looking Glass, and the shaman Toohoolhoozote refused, Howard gave them thirty days to comply. Although Joseph was in favour of peace, some of his warriors were not, and forced war upon their tribe by killing some white settlers. Pursued by Howard's troops and others in Montana, Joseph led his people across the mountains.

After fighting four pitched battles in a brilliantly-conducted 1700-mile, 108-day war of attrition and retreat, Joseph surrendered on October 5 with all his warriors in the Bear Paw mountains, just fifty miles south of the Canadian border and safety. Joseph's surrender speech is particularly moving, and as such is worth quoting in full:

> *I am tired of fighting. Our chiefs are killed. Looking Glass is dead. Toohulhulsote is dead. The old men are all dead. It is the young men who say yes or no. He who led the young men is dead. It is cold and we have no blankets. The little children are freezing to death. My people, some of them, have run away to the hills and have no blankets, no food. No one knows where they are – perhaps freezing to death. I want to have time to look for my children and see how many I can find. Maybe I shall find them among the dead. Hear me, my chiefs. I am tired. My heart is sick and sad. From where the sun now stands, I will fight no more forever.*

When the soldiers counted their prisoners of war they found that of the 750 Nez Percés who had fled the reservation on 15 June only 431 remained; of these only 79 were men. They begged to be returned to their own country, but General Sherman insisted they be treated severely and 'never allowed to return to Oregon.' As a result they were sent to reservations in Kansas, then the following year to Indian Territory. When eight years later they were returned to the northwest only 118 of the survivors were permitted to return to the old Nez Percé homeland. Chief Joseph never saw the Wallow valley again; he died – of a broken heart, according to the doctor who attended him – on 21 September 1904.

In 1878 it was the turn of the Bannocks; in 1878 and 1879 that of a desperately courageous band of Cheyennes led by Dull Knife and Little Wolf who broke out of their reservation in Indian Territory and tried to fight their way back to their homeland. In 1880 the Utes rose and were quashed. Only the Apaches, grim warriors of the unforgiving desert, held out any longer. But after the end of the Civil War, the US Army waged a war of attrition against them unlike any other. Its policy, as set down by Brigadier General James H. Carleton when he took over command of the Southwest, was short and stark:

The men are to be slain whenever and wherever they can be found. The women and children may be taken prisoner, but of course, they are not to be killed.

In 1865 alone, 363 Indians were killed and 140 wounded. Seven soldiers were killed in the same year, twenty-five wounded, with a further eighteen civilians dead and another thirteen wounded. Between 1866 and 1870, Apache warriors fought 137 separate engagements, many of them no more than skirmishes, others pitched battles. The army's pressure on the marauding Apaches became more and more severe as the months passed.

In 1871, Hackibanzin, better known to the whites as Eskiminzin, a leader of the Aravaipa Apaches, entered into surrender negotiations with Lieutenant Royal Whitman, 3rd Cavalry, and on 11 March more than 300 of his people were given asylum near Camp Grant, a US military post on the San Pedro River near Arivaipa Creek. Whitman put the Apaches to work cutting hay in return for food and shelter; this policy was so successful that within a few weeks there were over 500 Apaches at the camp.

During this same period, however, unidentified Apaches carried out a series of raids and killings in the Tucson area, and fanned by newspaper reports, Eskiminzin's people became prime suspects. The self-styled Tucson Committee of Public Safety led by Will Oury – six white men and forty-eight Mexicans aided by nearly a hundred Papago tribesmen, traditional enemies of the Apaches – started toward the post with the express intention of killing every Apache man, woman and child camped there. They attacked the sleeping camp on the morning of 30 April and when they were done, between 125 (Whitman's figure) and 144 (Oury's) Apaches had been slaughtered, only eight of them men. Army burial teams discovered that many of the women had been raped, others stabbed or their brains beaten out with stones. At one point a ten-month-old baby was found shot twice, one of its legs hacked off its tiny body. None of the Tucson mob was injured. Later it was discovered that the vigilantes had taken with them twenty-seven children who were sold into slavery; only six were ever returned.

The 'Camp Grant Massacre' as it became known raised such a storm of protest in the East that the perpetrators – including the Papagos – were arrested and put on trial in Tucson the following December. Although President Ulysses S. Grant had personally characterized the attack as 'purely murder' at the end of the five day trial the jury took exactly nineteen minutes to acquit the accused men.

It was not until 1872, largely through the efforts of his friend Thomas Jeffords, that Cochise agreed to talk peace with the US

Army and met General Oliver O. Howard, a one-armed, Bible-quoting veteran of the Civil War who convinced the Apache leader to renounce the warpath in return for a permanent reservation for the Chiricahua Apaches in the southeastern corner of the Territory which had always been their homeland. Henceforward, Cochise said, he would be at peace with the white man, and he kept his word until the day he died. But just to be on the safe side, President Grant had already appointed a new commander in Arizona. His name was George Crook.

Crook was a soldier's soldier. Born in 1829, he graduated from West Point in 1852 and took part in several Indian campaigns in the Northwest prior to the Civil War. His record in that conflict was exceptional. At the end of the War he was sent back to the Northwest where he won a reputation as a sensible, intelligent and sympathetic officer. The unconventional tactics he employed in his two-year campaign against the Paiute Indians effectively ended Indian resistance there.

Convinced the only way to fight the Apache was by fighting them with their own methods, he reorganized and retrained his command, employing 'friendly' Apache scouts to hunt their hostile cousins, and keeping constant pressure on the raiding bands.

By 1873, relative – but by no means perfect – peace had come to the Territory. Little by little, however, as more and more groups of young warriors turned 'bronco' and committed raids in Mexico and sometimes Arizona, and Crook was redeployed to the northern Plains to fight the Sioux, the 'peace' deteriorated. Then in 1876 the Bureau of Indian Affairs made one of the biggest mistakes in its history: it decreed that the Chiricahua Apaches be moved to the San Carlos reservation. This telegraphed order triggered a war of attrition more terrible than anything that had been seen before. Out of this conflict would come a new generation of Apache leaders. Juh,

Nana, Pionsenay, Victorio, Geronimo and others would outwit, outrun and outfight the entire US Army for nearly another ten years.

The Apaches could fight and they did. But they could never win, because unlike their opponents they were spending from a purse they could not refill: every warrior who was killed was irreplaceable. One by one their numbers were reduced, one by one their leaders were captured or killed. By 1885 only Geronimo was left, fighting a merciless guerilla war that would last until his final surrender in 1886 to General Nelson A. Miles. Unlike Crook, who had been in command since 1882, Miles made no attempt to rehabilitate Geronimo and his people. They were all sent in chains by train to Fort Marion, Florida and would never see their homeland again. As the train pulled out, the 4th Cavalry band played 'Auld Lang Syne.'

The long and tragic saga of the Indian wars came to an end in the bitter winter of 1890 with the Wounded Knee massacre, perhaps of all Indian fights the most controversial.

GHOSTS DANCING

Having spent a little over four years in Canadian exile, Sitting Bull was persuaded finally to return to American soil and surrender at Fort Buford, Montana on 19 July 1881. For two years he was a virtual prisoner at Fort Randall, but in 1883 he was permitted to return to his old home near the Standing Rock agency, where the agent was William McLaughlin.

For a while during 1885 Sitting Bull was permitted to travel with Buffalo Bill's Wild West Show; he returned to the agency, where he maintained his power over his people, much to the chagrin of the authorities who did not want there to be any Indian 'leaders.' His staunch opposition to the sale of reservation lands when the 1889 commission led by General Crook came to negotiate its purchase did nothing to make him more popular.

That same winter a new spirit took hold of the Sioux; it was said that an Indian Messiah had arisen. The word spread like wildfire among the oppressed Plains tribes and a great new religious fervour was born among them.

The Messiah was a Paiute named Wovoka. He had lived as a youth with white men, and so was also known as Jack Wilson. He was said to be the son of an earlier prophet, Tavibo, from whom he had learned the doctrines he now preached.

During an eclipse of the sun in 1889 Wovoka was stricken with a fever and during his illness dreamed he was taken to the afterworld to see the Supreme Being. He was told to return to the earth and tell his people to love one another and to live in peace with the white man. If they did this, and danced a ceremony the Supreme Being had given him, they would be reunited with all their friends in the other world, death would cease to be, the buffalo would return and the white man would disappear forever.

The Ghost Dance, as it was called, was inaugurated in the winter of 1889. By the following autumn the excitement this doctrine had raised among the Sioux was so intense it frightened a tyro Indian agent at the Pine Ridge agency so badly he called for troops, claiming the Indians were on the verge of an outbreak. When the troops arrived on 19 October 1890, huge numbers of Indians took to the Bad Lands; panicked settlers fled their homes as newspapers trumpeted the story of the Ghost Dance, but as yet there was no actual trouble. Indeed, agent McLaughlin issued a reassuring statement that there was no danger from his Indians. Sitting Bull remained quietly in his home on Grand River; he seems to have not taken any part in the new religion.

November passed without incident, but when word came in from a friendly Sioux that there was an encampment of more than two thousand Indians on the Cheyenne River, and Sitting Bull asked for a pass to go to Pine Ridge, General Nelson Miles decided on preemptive action: Sitting Bull must be arrested and the Indians disarmed.

At dawn on 15 December a hundred-strong detachment of cavalry commanded by Captain E. G. Fechét reached Grand River. A squad of forty-three Indian police surrounded Sitting Bull's cabin. Lieutenant Bull Head went into the cabin, roused the old man and told him he was under arrest. By this time Sioux Ghost Dancers were swarming like hornets around the cabin and as the policemen tried to hustle Sitting Bull to his horse one of his adherents, Catch-the-Bear, shot policeman Bull Head. As he fell, Bull Head shot Sitting Bull through the body. Then Sergeant Red Tomahawk shot him through the head, killing him.

Suddenly everyone was shooting. The Indian police took shelter in Sitting Bull's cabin, killing his 17-year-old son as they ran in. Now Captain Fechét got into the action, unlimbering the Hotchkiss gun he had brought with him from Fort Yates and opened fire. When the shooting stopped four policemen and eight Hunkpapa Sioux were dead as well as Sitting Bull. His head smashed in by the vengeful Indian police, Sitting Bull was buried in an unmarked grave – in quicklime.

Now it was time to disarm the Indians on Cherry Creek. On 17 December orders were issued for the arrest of Big Foot, one of the 'fomentors of disturbances.' In fact, as soon as Big Foot had heard of the death of Sitting Bull he had started his people for Pine Ridge, but he fell ill with pneumonia and had to travel in a wagon.

Nearly three thousand troops were deployed to find and capture Big Foot's people and on December 28, Major Samuel Whitside intercepted the Minneconjous near Porcupine Creek. Although he had orders to disarm and dismount all the Indians, Whitside took the advice of his scout John Shangreau who feared that if the soldiers tried to take their arms the Indians would fight, and escorted them instead to Wounded Knee Creek – the same area in which Crazy Horse's parents had buried the heart of their son.

When they reached the cavalry tent camp the Indians were counted: 120 men, 230 women and children. Rations were issued and tents provided, but to make sure none of the prisoners escaped Whitside posted two Hotchkiss guns on a rise overlooking the encampment. Later that night the remainder of the 7th Cavalry came in and Colonel James W. Forsyth, commanding, took charge. After placing two more Hotchkiss guns next to Whitside's, the soldiers settled down with a keg of whiskey to celebrate the capture of the 'hostiles'.

The following morning after surrounding the camp with a ring of soldiers – not a few of them seasoned veterans of the US Army's Indian wars – Forsyth issued the Indians with hardtack for breakfast then informed them they were to be disarmed. After they had complied by surrendering their weapons, the soldiers searched all the tipis confiscating knives, tomahawks, even tent stakes, and then body searches were conducted.

At this juncture the medicine man, Yellow Bird, began to dance the Ghost Dance and chanted that he had made medicine of the white men's ammunition, and that his bullets would not penetrate the Indians' ghost shirts, while their bullets would kill.

What happened next is the subject of violent disagreement between witnesses on both sides. It appears, however, that only two weapons were found during the body searches, one a new Winchester belonging to a young warrior named Black Coyote, who at first refused to turn it over, and then after one of the soldiers tried to take it from him, fired it. And then all hell broke loose.

The Minneconjou were helplessly grouped together inside a circle of soldiers, and had nowhere to run when the military opened fire. Big Foot was among the first killed, but there were many more. Then as the Indians tried to break through the circle of soldiers, hand-to-hand fighting broke out. Then the Hotchkiss guns opened up, firing explosive shells into the massed Indians and creating fearful casualties. 'We tried to run,' said a survivor, 'but they shot at us like we were buffalo.'

When the shooting stopped and the smoke cleared, more than half of Big Foot's people were dead or seriously wounded. Official figures later put the number of Indian known dead at 146 (including 44 women and 18 children) and 51 known wounded (only four of whom were men). The Army had 25 men killed and 39 wounded.

The 'battle' of Wounded Knee brought to an end the long, sad story of the Indian Wars and perhaps even more tragically, the end of the Indian dream. No one ever expressed it better than the Oglala Sioux holy man Black Elk (1863–1950):

> I did not know then how much was ended. When I look back now from the high hill of my old age, I can still see the butchered women and children lying heaped and scattered all along the crooked gulch as plain as when I saw them with eyes still young. And I can see that something else died there in the bloody mud, and was buried in the blizzard. A people's dream died there. It was a beautiful dream [but] there is no centre any longer, and the sacred tree is dead.

No comprehensive statistical record of the Indian Wars exists. One US Army compilation listed 1005 engagements between 1866 and 1891, but it does not claim to be complete, since some of these fights were between civilians and Indians. Of 930 recorded fights between soldiers and Indians, 592 involved small detachments; in only 70 were five companies or more engaged. The largest number of engagements in a single year was 140 in 1868. Altogether 932 soldiers were killed and 1061 wounded between 1866 and 1891.

How many Indians died in those wars no one will ever know. What the human cost of them was, no one can ever say, although Secretary of War Robert Todd Lincoln estimated that between 1872 and 1882 alone, Indian campaigning cost the government nearly $224 million. Today that would be approximately $20 billion, or $200 million for each and every year of that decade. Multiply that in turn by the number of years the white man fought the Indian – from 1789 to 1891 – and the figure becomes unimaginable.

How much the land of which the Indians were systematically robbed by the white man would be worth today, no one can begin to estimate. Only one thing can be said for sure: the descendants of those Indians remain to this day the most economically deprived minority in American life. As Sioux leader Red Cloud bitterly observed toward the end of his life, 'The white men made us many promises, more than I can remember, but they never kept but one; they promised to take our land, and they took it.'

The Wild Bunch. *Seated left to right:* Harry A. Longabaugh, alias the Sundance Kid; Ben Kilpatrick, alias the Tall Texan; Robert Leroy Parker, alias Butch Cassidy. *Standing:* Will Carver; Harvey Logan, alias Kid Curry. Photograph taken in Fort Worth, Texas, 1901.

CHAPTER TEN

THE LAST FRONTIER

BY THE TIME the 7th Cavalry's merciless Hotchkiss guns slaughtered Big Foot and his tribesmen at Wounded Knee, enormous changes had taken place all across the West. States like Kansas, Iowa, Minnesota, Nebraska and Missouri were 'settled up', all the available land filed on and under cultivation. On the open cattle ranges of the Southwest and in Montana and Wyoming, too, further changes were in progress.

They might be said to have begun when the mechanical refrigeration already widely used on railroads was adapted for use in seagoing vessels, and cheap American beef began to compete in England with the superior, but much more expensive, home-grown variety. The year-on-year increase in these imports became so great that (on a sort of 'if you can't beat them, join them' basis) Scottish meat raisers interested themselves in the American cattle trade.

When James MacDonald, a reporter from the agricultural newspaper *The Scotsman*, first investigated and then produced a book about it, followed by a government report on Texas ranching that suggested it could yield annual profits of 33 per cent, that initially academic interest became a fever of excitement that swiftly swept through England (and more especially Scotland) as well as – spurred on there by similar books and reports – the eastern cities of the USA.

What became known as 'the beef bonanza' was about to begin.

Once the amazing British romance with the American cattle industry began, an almost unbelievable flood of money poured – much of it English, but even more from Scotland – into America in general and Texas in particular. Texas was attractive to investors for two reasons: not only had it moved directly from independence to statehood without the intervening inconvenience of Territorial status, but in doing so it had retained control of all its public land. Thus it would not only be possible but practical in 1885 for an investment company to make a deal with the State – not the Federal government – under the terms of which it would erect a $3 million capitol building in Austin in exchange for three million acres of land in the Texas Panhandle. The result was the XIT Ranch – which, as every cowboy knew, was shorthand for the ten counties in Texas over which its enormous herds ranged.

The Capitol Syndicate which made that deal may have been the biggest, but it was not by any means the first company to invest in the new bonanza. It is said that in 1882 alone some £6,000,000 (then $30 million, now more like $200–300 million) was invested in Texas by British cattle companies. In Scotland, the Scottish-American Mortgage Co. bought up George W. Littlefield's LIT Ranch in the Panhandle and some adjoining spreads in New Mexico, consolidating their purchases into the a huge syndicated ranching organization called the Prairie Land & Cattle Company, with herds in the region of 150,000 head.

That same year, after similar wholesale purchases of land and cattle in Texas and elsewhere, further syndicates: the Matador Land & Cattle Company (headquartered in Dundee), the Hansford Land & Cattle Co., the Cedar Valley Cattle Co., the Wyoming Cattle Co., the Cattle Ranche Co., and the Rocking Chair Ranche – whose principal owners included Sir Dudley Marjoribanks, the first Baron

Tweedsmouth and John C. Hamilton Gordon, 7th Earl of Aberdeen – were formed. In Wyoming the Swan Land and Cattle Company, also financed with British money, grazed its herds on a range that stretched westward from Ogallala, Nebraska to Fort Steele and south from the UP transcontinental line to the Platte River.

Within a very short space of time the whole business of cattle ranching – and by definition cowboying – changed radically. It became a business, run by absentee corporations and syndicates, managed by men employed as much if not more for their financial acumen than their ability to 'tally' a herd, men who frowned upon the old free-and-easy open range traditions and insisted on industry-agreed pay scales and scheduled working hours. Even more contentiously, the new administrators declared taboo the old tradition that permitted cowboys to slap their own brands on any mavericks – unbranded calves – they encountered in their daily work and add them to their own little herd.

The cowboys, needless to say, not only strongly objected to these strictures but refused to obey them. The more the syndicates tried to enforce them, the greater became the resistance, and the end result was the abortive cowboy strike of 1883 in the Texas Panhandle, when the 'hired hands' rebelled against the growing power of the syndicates. They never really had a chance. Strikers were black-listed; unable to get work many of them turned full-time rustler, while others staked out homesteads just a few miles across the state line in New Mexico (where Texas law couldn't touch them) and without compunction began building up herds of their own at the expense of their former employers.

In the Panhandle, unable to overcome the reluctance of juries to hand down indictments against 'the little men' the big companies hired Pat Garrett, still riding high on his reputation as the man who killed Billy the Kid, to lead a force of 'Rangers' that would stop the rustling, but it was disbanded after a year. The resentments fuelled by these actions eventually exploded in a murderous gunfight at Tascosa, the self-styled 'Cowboy Capital of the Panhandle' on a moonlit Saturday night in March, 1886 in which four men were killed and two others badly wounded.

Resistance to change could do nothing to prevent it, however. By that same summer of 1886, the era of free grass was over; open range grazing was virtually a thing of the past. The old practice of turning cattle loose to graze free in the Indian Territory, later to become Oklahoma, was banned by Presidential decree. Barbed wire soon closed in every major ranch – and as a result anyone who did not own his land was doomed. Rising beef prices had encouraged overstocking and there simply was no longer enough grass to feed the millions of cattle roaming free on the high plains from Saskatchewan to Texas.

Then disaster struck: in the winter of 1886 a blizzard raged down from Canada straight through to the Gulf of Mexico. For two weeks it rained; then it froze hard, and then it began to snow. It was one of the worst storms anyone on the high plains had ever experienced, with the lowest temperatures ever recorded. Unable to find either food or water, half a million cattle died in Montana and Wyoming alone. In Texas thousands more piled up against the barbed wire fences and froze to death. The gaunt survivors dumped on the market by ranchers desperate for cash the following spring were in such poor condition that prices fell sharply, accelerating the slide to ruin of the few men who had not been wiped out the previous winter. The larger syndicates with their huge investment reserves just about held on, but the smaller men were finished: to this day cattlemen refer to the winter of 1886 as 'the Big Die.'

Over the six or eight years that followed as the ranching industry reorganized itself after the Big Die, a radical re-think took place. Cattle no longer grazed on open range but were kept in fenced pastures and fed during the winter. Ranchers no longer needed dozens of hired hands or big remudas of horses for them to patrol the range; trail bosses, chuckwagons and roundups became a thing of the past. More and more as law, order, politics, system and improvement spread and the free, wild, raw frontier was levelled and smoothed by the inevitable advent of civilization the once free-ranging cowboy became a farm hand. Many of them philosophically accepted the changes and adapted to them. Others joined the homesteaders who were flooding in and staked out spreads on the wide-open prairies they had once roamed. Not a few of them slapped their brands on any mavericks that happened to come their way.

As a result the cattle barons tarred all homesteaders with the same brush, calling them rustlers even though the majority of them were honest. The homesteaders, whether small ranchers or farmers, in turn refused to recognize the monopolies claimed by the bigger men, especially in the matter of land ownership. In the summer of 1889, in Johnson County, about 250 miles northwest of Cheyenne, a 'war' flared up between the nesters and the big and influential ranchers of Wyoming. The Wyoming ranchers, after suffering several years of losing cattle to rustlers the courts never seemed able to punish, decided to take the law into their own hands.

THE JOHNSON COUNTY WAR

The incident which precipitated the conflict, a down-and-dirty lynching, took place on 20 July 1889, when a group of cattlemen seized two homesteaders who lived on adjoining claims. The victims were ex-infantryman James Averell, a justice of the peace who ran a store and saloon but owned no cattle, and his common law wife Ella Lidday Andrews, who was known as Cattle Kate because (it was alleged) she traded her favours for unbranded cattle.

Averell, the acknowledged leader of the smaller ranchers in the

Sweetwater Valley, had written letters to and articles for local news-papers protesting against the high-handed methods of the bigger men who had passed a 'Maverick Bill' by which all unbranded cattle found on the range were deemed the property of the Stockmen's Association, to be confiscated by its minions.

By taking this stance, Averell fell foul of rancher Albert J. Both-well, 'largest and most arrogant of the local big stockmen,' who claimed Averell and Andrews were occupying land that belonged to him. On 20 July 1889 a six man 'posse' led by Bothwell arrived at Cattle Kate's place and 'arrested' them. Without even the pretence of a trial or a hearing they were taken by wagon to a lonely canyon and hanged. Two witnesses to the hanging later disappeared without trace; a third left hastily for England. No one was ever indicted or arrested for the crime because the men involved were themselves the highest authority in Wyoming.

For a while the resentments of these powerful men – with the renowned Cheyenne Club as their headquarters, the hundred members of the Wyoming Live Stock Association owned over two million head of cattle – continued to simmer without actually boiling over, perhaps held in place by the fact that the little red-headed Sheriff, William G. Angus, was no admirer of the big corporations.

A couple of years later, however, 'emboldened by exemption from prosecution' (to quote a contemporary chronicler) in the deaths of Averell and Cattle Kate, the big ranchers embarked upon an undeclared war against the rustlers. First to go was Tom Wag-goner, another small rancher, who was arrested and taken from his cabin on 4 June 1891. His body was found eight days later in a nearby gully, hanged by the vigilantes. A few months later, on 1 November 1891, an (alleged) attempt was made to kill former trail boss Nathan D. Champion and his ranching partner Ross Gilbertson as they slept. Considered by the big ranchers to be a leading light in the 'Hole in the Wall gang' of rustlers, Champion by his own account fought the four attackers off, apparently wounding one.

In quick succession two other small ranchers, O. E. 'Ranger' Jones and John Tisdale, were ambushed and assassinated. Some historians believe Champion's story about the attempt on his life was fiction; that in fact he, Jones, Tisdale and perhaps others had been involved in a shootout with a group of syndicate supporters led by former Texas badman Joe Horner. Horner, a bank robber and shootist now going under the name of Frank Canton, was arrested in connection with the attack on Champion and the killing of Tisdale, but posted bail and walked free. It would certainly explain the otherwise seemingly motiveless assassinations of Tisdale and Jones.

The ensuing 'Johnson County War' pitted syndicate vigilantes and hired guns led by Canton against the nesters and smaller ranchers. Calling themselves 'Invaders' (yet another term for Regulators) and said to have been financed by a $100,000 fund raised by the members of the Cheyenne Club, forty-six vigilantes led by Frank Canton backed by nineteen cattlemen, twenty-odd hired guns from Texas and five stock detectives (and even two newspapermen!) assembled at Denver and were brought by special train to Cheyenne. Their avowed intention was to take over Johnson County, suppress the local law, and wipe out the rustlers.

Informed that Nick Ray and Nate Champion, two men they particularly wanted, were at a nearby ranch, this small army abandoned its plan to invade and take over Buffalo and instead made a detour fourteen miles to the north where, on the morning of 9 April they surrounded Nolan's KC ranch. Two trappers who were staying in the three-room cabin were captured as they emerged. After a while Nick Ray came out and was shot down without warning. Nate Champion dashed out and amid a hail of lead dragged his mortally wounded comrade back into the cabin.

For the rest of the morning and most of the afternoon, under a constant and relentless barrage of gunfire, Champion held off the entire attacking force, at the same time comforting the dying Ray who had been hit in the head and body. Throughout the day he jotted down in a little memorandum book one of the most amazing 'eyewitness accounts' ever written:

> *It is now about two hours since the first shot. Nick is still alive; they are still shooting and are all around the house. Boys, there is bullets coming in like hail.*

Ray died about nine o'clock, wrote Champion. And later:

> *Boys, I feel pretty lonesome just now. I wish there was someone here with me so we could watch all sides at once ... It's about 3 o'clock now. There was a man in a buckboard and one on horseback just passed. They fired on them as they went by.*

The posse had been surprised by a local farmer returning home. When they turned their guns on him he fled, abandoning his wagon. This was commandeered, loaded with hay and pitch pine, dragged to the rear window, and set on fire. Champion knew his situation was hopeless. 'It's not night yet,' he wrote. 'The house is all fired. Goodbye, boys, if I never see you again.' Then he picked up his Winchester and made a run from the blazing shack. He was shot down without mercy. Twenty-eight bullets were found in his body, to which a note had been pinned:

CATTLE THIEVES BEWARE

Now the Invaders marched on Buffalo, the intention to strike before daylight, capturing the town and killing off the opposition, notably Sheriff 'Red' Angus. But as they approached the town word reached them that the Sheriff, his deputies, and a party of two hundred armed citizens was waiting for them. Canton and his men decided to back off and instead dig in at the nearby TA Ranch on Crazy Woman Creek and they were just in time. A large party of citizens surrounded them, capturing their wagons.

For the next two days they laid siege to the ranch and then, impatient with the standoff, the attackers determined to build a contraption they called a 'Go-Devil,' which consisted of two of the captured wagons with logs lashed together to form a moveable barrier that could be pushed down the hill under cover of darkness until it got near enough for the men inside to throw dynamite into the house.

Before this plan could be effected, however, three troops of cavalry under the command of Colonel James J. Van Horn arrived from Fort McKinney and under a flag of truce, brought the battle to an end and effected the surrender of the vigilantes. Only two of the Invaders had been wounded in the siege; one later died.

It transpired later that one of the Invaders had slipped out of the TA during the night and got word to the Governor of Wyoming and it was he who had called out the troops to protect the Invaders: the big men were protecting their own. Taken to Cheyenne to avoid their being handed over to Sheriff Angus, the prisoners were brought to trial on 21 January 1893. It was a puppet show. The two trappers who had witnessed the killing of Champion and Ray were induced with threats and cheques (later to prove worthless) to leave the State and in the absence of evidence against the defendants, all charges were dismissed.

For all that there were further ambushes and assassinations until it sputtered to its inconclusive end. The Johnson County War is notable because it was the high-water mark of the dominance of the cattle barons and the new West of the homesteader just as, in a totally different way, the rise and fall of the Wyoming 'Wild Bunch' and its two most famous members, Butch Cassidy and the Sundance Kid, marks the line between the early gunfighters and bandits and what was effectively to be the last of the breed.

BUTCH AND SUNDANCE

Butch Cassidy's real name was Robert LeRoy Parker. The son of a solid Mormon family who had crossed the plains on foot as 'hand-cart pioneers' in 1856, he was born in Beaver, Utah, on Friday, 13 April 1866 and raised on his father's ranch near Circleville. As a teenager he became friendly with Mike Cassidy, a cowboy who taught young Bob how to ride and rope and shoot, not to mention how to quietly rustle a maverick to supplement your income.

Cassidy and Parker left Utah and drifted down to Telluride, where they fell in with a couple of small-time bandits, Matt Warner and Tom McCarty, both of whom were also from Mormon families. On 29 June 1889, aided perhaps by his brother Dan and Bill Madden, Butch (nobody knows where he got the nickname from) helped them to rob the mining town's San Miguel Valley Bank of around $20,000. It might fairly be said this was the genesis of the amorphous gang that would become known as the Wild Bunch, although Butch Cassidy (young Robert Parker had by now borrowed his mentor's name for an alias) seems to have been something of a part-time member at this stage.

And what about the Sundance Kid? Contrary to movie legend, he and Butch were not an inseparable pair from the start; indeed, they did not even team up until 1896 at the earliest and possibly not even until the turn of the century. Nor did either of them ever have a traditional gunfight, bar-room brawl or showdown – in fact, they seem to have taken great pains to avoid shooting anyone. Harry Longabaugh, to give the Sundance Kid the name he was born with in 1867, was from Pennsylvania. He came west with a cousin's family around 1882, and after being arrested for horse theft in 1887 spent eighteen months in jail at Sundance, Wyoming, which is where the nickname came from.

While Sundance was in Canada and Butch was in limbo, Tom McCartney, his brothers Bill and George (plus George's wife Nellie) and his nephew Fred, Matt Warner and Hank Vaughan pulled off a series of holdups in Oregon, Washington, and Colorado. Their crime spree ended in 1893 when Fred and Bill were killed during a raid on a bank in Delta, Colorado.

Sundance reappears in 1892 in a botched attempt to hold up a train near Malta, Montana. His partners Bill Madden and Harry Bass were captured; the Kid got away with maybe $100 and disappeared from the historical record for almost a decade. Butch, who had been out of sight, perhaps enjoying his share of the proceeds from the Telluride robbery, popped up briefly in 1892 to be sentenced to two years in prison for the theft of a $5 horse. In 1896 he joined Elza Lay and Bob Meeks in the robbery of the Bank of Montpelier, Idaho, getting away with over $7000, which the outlaws brazenly claimed was to pay the legal costs of their buddy Matt Warner, who was on trial for murder.

So it becomes clear that the Wild Bunch – also known over the years as the Hole-in-the-Wall Gang, the Train Robbers Syndicate, Butch Cassidy's gang, Kid Curry's gang, the Powder Springs gang and the Robbers Roost gang – was something of a freemasonry with a constantly-changing membership. At that time, the Sundance Kid remained relatively unknown; it was Butch who got all the headlines. The 'King of the Bandits' as one Chicago paper called him, was not just any badman, but 'the worst man' in four states, leader of a gang consisting of 500 outlaws subdivided into five smaller bands. In actual fact, as the following timeline shows, Butch and Sundance were simply not in the same league as such outlaws as Jesse and Frank James.

THE WILD BUNCH: A CAREER HISTORY

21 April 1897

Butch Cassidy, Elza Lay, and two other men steal a $9,800 mine payroll at Castle Gate, Utah.

26 July 1897

Bandits George 'Flat Nose' Currie, Harvey 'Kid Curry' Logan, Walt Pulteney, Tom O'Day and the Sundance Kid (and just possibly Butch) bungle a bank robbery at Belle Fourche, South Dakota, getting away with less than $100.

14 July 1898

Three bandits said to have been Sundance, Logan and Currie hold up a Southern Pacific train at Humboldt, Nevada, escaping with $450.

3 April 1899

The same trio are alleged to have robbed a saloon in Elko, Nevada, but it seems likelier that the three local cowboys who were arrested, tried and released were the real culprits.

December 1900

Butch, Sundance, Will Carver, Ben Kilpatrick 'the tall Texan' and Harvey Logan, dressed to the nines, have their photo taken in a group at El Paso, Texas. This turns out to have been one of the biggest mistakes they ever made, because the Pinkerton Detective Agency obtains a copy of the photo and from that day on all of them are marked men.

THE LAST FRONTIER

20 February 1901

Butch, Sundance and Sundance's friend Etta Place sail for Argentina. On arrival, using the names James 'Santiago' Ryan, Harry and Ethel Place, they deposit $12,000 in gold notes (about $250,000 in today's money) in a Buenos Aires bank.

June 1901

The trio settle on a ranch in the Cholila Valley, record a brand and buy livestock. Accused of a bank robbery that was probably committed by two other 'bandidos Yanqui', they flee to Chile (probably to avoid identification by the Pinkertons, who are still on their case).

19 December 1905

Butch, Sundance and two others (maybe Etta Place and cowboy Bob Evans from Cholila) hold up a bank in Villa Mercedes, Argentina and escape in a wild shootout. After this Etta leaves for America and disappears. Butch and Sundance go to Bolivia and work for a while at the Concordia tin mine.

4 November 1908

Butch and Sundance steal a mine payroll near Tupiza in southern Bolivia. Two days later on 6 November they are trapped by a small military patrol in a village named San Vicente, high in the Andes. According to the best evidence available, Butch shoots Sundance and then kills himself; the payroll is recovered intact among their possessions.

Perhaps there is a wry irony in the fact that of all the imaginary exploits screenwriter William Goldman invented for the movie Butch Cassidy and the Sundance Kid, it was in the final scene that he probably came as near as he ever got to the truth.

Outlawry was never going to go away, of course, but it would never be the same after the turn of the century. The world had changed. There were no more stagecoaches to hold up. Banks and trains were no longer easy targets. Large sums of money were now transported in armoured cars. More importantly, law enforcement had changed, and in the changing become infinitely more sophisticated. Horseback bandits with clumsy, inaccurate Colt .45s were no match for law officers or federal agents with machine guns. Telephones, telegraphs, photographs, fast trains (by 1900 it took only twenty-four hours to get from New York to Chicago instead of the fifty hours it had taken in 1860) and soon even the automobile – Henry Ford built his first car in a shed in Detroit in June, 1896 – could and would be mobilized to pursue criminals.

The frontier was gone, and with it the day of the explorer, the scout, the wild Apache and Cheyenne, the gunfighter and the outlaw, was over. Soon the wide swathes of the cattle trails would disappear, to be replaced by endless stands of waving wheat or corn. Even the deep-cut ruts ground into the rocky earth by the wagon trains would fade, their paths remembered only in historical markers.

Today you can follow the routes those wagons took – even the trails Lewis and Clark took – from historical marker to tourist signpost, covering in hours in your air-conditioned car distances that took the explorers and emigrants weeks to traverse. Along each highway there are reconstructed forts and buildings, museums, historical societies, battlefield markers, State parks, National parks. But only rarely the real thing any more. On Deadwood's Main Street, where Calamity Jane strutted and Wild Bill Hickok played his last game of cards, every building is either a casino (one of them owned by Kevin Costner – this is *Dances with Wolves* country) a restaurant (Kevin owns one of those, too) or a souvenir store. There's even a shop where you can buy a complete buffalo hide and a museum where you can see the original Deadwood stage. Near Buffalo, you can see the KC ranch where plucky Nate Champion died in the Johnson County War, and there's a brilliant museum in Buffalo full of mementoes of those bloody days. You can drive from the replica Fort Phil Kearny to the marker on the top of the ridge above where Crazy Horse's warriors massacred Fetterman's cavalry. You can see the truly incredible array of Western guns and memorabilia collected by the Buffalo Bill Museum in Cody.

You can sign up to do a wagon train drive on the Oregon Trail. You can ride horseback across the Little Big Horn battlefield. You can visit Jesse James's grave or stand on the banks of the American River almost exactly where James Marshall found the traces of gold that started the California Gold Rush. You can spend a week or two 'cowboying' on a dude ranch. You can see the annual corn dance performed in a New Mexico pueblo much as it was five centuries ago. You can visit location after location, each one echoing with history, in almost every State west of the Mississippi, but somehow... somehow in nearly all these places where the Old West ought to be, it just isn't there.

The Alamo still stands, a tiny little island in the centre of the huge, bustling city of San Antonio, surrounded by high rise office buildings and hotels that have long since buried the one-time sprawl of outbuildings where Bowie died and Travis fell and most of the famous battle took place. The fact that nearly all the fighting took place outside it is of course not emphasized, for otherwise the building itself would be, and for most of its visitors generally is, just another vacation-photo opportunity. The chapel itself – a powder magazine then – is a Texan shrine, the atmosphere reverential, every exhibit a relic – anyone misguided enough to wear a hat indoors or shout 'Yee-haw' the way Davy Crockett might have done, would soon be given cause indeed to remember the Alamo.

At the Little Big Horn battlefield, visitors no longer explore the footpaths on the humpy hills where George Armstrong Custer and his cavalrymen made their last, desperate stand. Instead throngs of them in shorts and T-shirts toil up the path to the monument at the top of the hill, take photos and leave. Some drive the few miles along the crest of the ridge to where Reno and Benteen dug in, but the sheer presence of so many people and so many cars make it impossible for anyone to appreciate the dynamics of the battle – how they died, why they died. In the museum they have one of Custer's uniforms and everyone goes Gosh, he wasn't very tall.

Near Kearney, Missouri, you can visit the farm in which Jesse James was born and see Frank James's duster coat hanging on a peg behind the door. Outside in the yard you can take a picture of the tombstone his embittered mother erected above Jesse's grave, commemorating the son 'murdered by a traitor and a coward whose name is not worthy to appear here'. It's a replica: the real one was chipped to pieces by tourists half a century ago, and anyway, Jesse is buried in the cemetery in town. In St Joseph you can step into the actual house (relocated from its original site) in which Bob Ford assassinated Jesse James. When they show you the hole in the wall made by the bullet that killed him, don't mention the autopsy that showed it remained lodged in his brain.

The cattle towns – Abilene, Wichita, Ellsworth, Dodge City and the rest, still trade mightily on the trail driving days, and each has its 'replica cowtown' – although to give them credit the good burghers of Abilene also offer the visitor a museum dedicated to another distinguished native son, former President Dwight D. Eisenhower. No sadder and less historically accurate memorial to the Old West exists than Dodge's replica Front Street, which is not only sited several hundred yards away from the actual location (now a parking lot) but actually celebrates with stunningly impartial inaccuracy in its 'Long

Branch Saloon' (soft drinks only) the exploits of Wyatt Earp and Doc Holliday on the one hand, and Marshal Matt Dillon and Miss Kitty on the other, an unforgiveable blurring of historical reality and television which seems to perturb neither the hordes of visitors who traipse through the place every summer nor the city fathers who take their dollars.

Tombstone is better, but that's about it. Get there early, before the stores open and the tourist machine starts up, and it can look startlingly like it did in the 1880s, but by the time the sun is halfway up the sky, Tombstone is Old West tourist hell, with western-dressed touts on every street corner selling tickets for a ride around town on the stagecoach or one of the stunt-man 'gunfights' that seem to take place every hour on the hour. The saloons and gambling houses where Doc Holliday dealt poker and Wyatt Earp busted Clanton heads are pale imitations of the originals although late in the evening when they're lit up and noisy, they emit a hint of what it might have been like back then. The tacky sham of 'the OK Corral' with its pathetically unconvincing statues purportedly 'marking the spot' where the gunfight took place is so awful you can't believe they did it, and anyway, the fight was on Frémont Street, now the main highway through town.

In Billy the Kid country, the highway running from Roswell to Ruidoso bisects the village of Lincoln, New Mexico – population today less than a hundred souls – much as the enmity of the two opposing factions split it in 1878. Thankfully, the place hasn't been 're-imagined' and still looks much as it did in the Kid's time. A Pat Garrett hotel, a museum, a couple of bed and breakfast hotels and an annual 'Billy the Kid Pageant' are about the only concessions made to visitors. Clump up the stairs in the old Murphy-Dolan store, now a State Monument, and it's not hard to imagine the Kid at the top killing one of the deputies who were guarding him. Down the street stands the store built by John Tunstall; just across from it is the spot where Sheriff Brady and his deputy were gunned down. Nearby an open patch of dusty ground marks the spot where 'the big killing' of 1878 happened. The Kid himself is elsewhere, 150 miles northeast at Fort Sumner. His gravestone has for the last thirty years been protected by an iron cage so tourists can't chip pieces off it for souvenirs. If you want to 'feel' the past a little more realistically, go there at twilight.

But most of all, go. Go if only to see the incredible expanses of it, the sometimes unbelievable beauty of the landscape and the rackety awfulness of some of the towns in which so many hundreds of thousands of these events were set, so many hopes and aspirations and ambitions blossomed, so many untold stories still remain untold. Take enough imagination, and the Old West can still be found out there, down some canyon, over some mountain, along some river.

There never was anywhere quite like it. And there never will be again.

A stagecoach is attacked by Indians in this classic Western scene by Frederic Remington (1861–1909).

RECOMMENDED READING

Although it makes no claim to be comprehensive, this selection from the vast number of books dealing with the many and different aspects of the history of the American West has been chosen primarily for their availability in reasonably-priced form. Paperback editions are indicated with a (P), hardcover editions with an (H), and high priced hardcover and/or 'collector's items' with a (C). They are listed in order of usefulness.

Western Americana is avidly collected in hardback and some of the 'classics' or even more recent books which were published in small runs that went quickly out of print inevitably command higher prices. The reader is strongly recommended to check for copies of these books on what is in the author's opinion the best secondhand book website on the Internet: www.abebooks.com.

CHAPTER 1: TRAILBLAZERS

Leroy R. Hafen (ed.). *The Mountain Men and the Fur Trade of the Far West: Biographical Sketches of the Participants.* 10 vols.

Arthur H. Clarke Co. 1965–71. (C)

J. Cecil Alter. *Jim Bridger.* University of Oklahoma Press. (P)

John C. Frémont. *Narratives of Exploration and Adventure.* Longmans Green. (H)

James P. Ronda. *Lewis and Clark Among the Indians.* University of Nebraska Press. (P)

THE WILD WEST

Stephen Ambrose. *Undaunted Courage: Meriwether Lewis, Thomas Jefferson and the Opening of the American West.* Simon & Schuster NY. (P)

Harold P. Howard. *Sacajawea.* University of Oklahoma Press. (P)

Dale L. Morgan. *Jedediah Smith and the Opening of the West.* University of Nebraska Press. (P)

CHAPTER 2: THE WAY WEST

Bill Groneman. *Eyewitness to the Alamo.* Republic of Texas Press. (P)

Lon Tinkle. *The Alamo: Thirteen Days to Glory.* McGraw-Hill NY. (C)

Walter Lord. *A Time to Stand: The Epic of the Alamo.* University of Nebraska Press. (P)

George R. Stewart, *Ordeal by Hunger: The Story of the Donner Party.* University of Nebraska Press. (P)

Francis Parkman. *The Oregon Trail.* University of Nebraska Press. (P)

CHAPTER 3: FIGHTING INDIANS

Stan Hoig. *The Sand Creek Massacre.* University of Oklahoma Press. (P)

George Bird Grinnell. *The Fighting Cheyennes.* University of Oklahoma Press. (P)

Martin E Schmitt, (ed.). *General George Crook: His Autobiography.* University of Oklahoma Press. (P)

George A. Custer. *My Life on the Plains.* University of Oklahoma Press. (P)

Edgar I. Stewart. *Custer's Luck.* University of Oklahoma Press. (P)

Robert M. Utley. *Cavalier in Buckskin: George Armstrong Custer and the Western Military Frontier.* University of Oklahoma Press. (P)

——. *The Lance and the Shield: The Life and Times of Sitting Bull.* Ballantine. (P)

Larry McMurtry. *Crazy Horse.* Penguin. (P)

CHAPTER 4: COWTOWNS AND GUNSMOKE

Andy Adams. *The Log of a Cowboy*. University of Nebraska Press. (P)

E. C. Abbott ('Teddy Blue') *We Pointed Them North*. University of Oklahoma Press. (P)

Wayne Gard. *The Chisholm Trail*. University of Oklahoma Press. (P)

Joseph G. Rosa. *They Called Him Wild Bill*. University of Oklahoma Press. (P)

Stanley Vestal. *Dodge City: Queen of Cowtowns*. University of Nebraska Press. (P)

Nyle H. Miller & Joseph Snell. *Great Gunfighters of the Kansas Cowtowns,1867–1886*. University of Nebraska Press. (P)

Wayne Gard. *The Chisholm Trail*. University of Oklahoma Press. (P)

Robert K. De Arment. *Bat Masterson: The Man and the Legend* University of Oklahoma Press. (P)

CHAPTER 5: TO THE LAST MAN

Leon C. Metz. *John Wesley Hardin, Dark Angel of Texas*. University of Oklahoma Press. (P)

Hardin, John Wesley. *The Life of ... As Written by Himself*. University of Oklahoma Press. (P)

Robert N. Mullin,(ed.). *Maurice Garland Fulton's History of the Lincoln County War*. University of Arizona Press. (P)

Frederick Nolan. *The Lincoln County War: A Documentary History*. University of Oklahoma Press. (P)

—. *The West of Billy the Kid.* University of Oklahoma Press. (P)

—. *Bad Blood: The Life and Times of the Horrell Brothers*. Barbed Wire Press. (H)

Bob Boze Bell. *The Illustrated Life and Times of Billy the Kid*. Tri-Star Boze Publications. (P)

C. L. Sonnichsen. *Ten Texas Feuds*. University of New Mexico Press. (C)

—. *I'll Die Before I Run*. Devin-Adair NY. (C)

Don Dedera. *A Little War of Our Own*. Northland Press, Flagstaff. (C)

Earle R. Forrest. *Arizona's Dark and Bloody Ground*. Caxton, Idaho. (C)

CHAPTER 6: GOLD, SILVER...AND LEAD

Robert M. Coates. *The Outlaw Years: The Bandits of the Natchez Trace.* University of Nebraska Press. (P)

Thomas J. Dimsdale. *The Vigilantes of Montana.* University of Oklahoma Press. (P)

R. E. Mather & F. E. Boswell. *Gold Camp Desperadoes: Violence, Crime and Punishment on the Mining Frontier.* University of Oklahoma Press. (P)

John Boessenecker. *Lawman: The Life and Times of Harry Morse, 1855–1912.* University of Oklahoma Press. (P)

Karen Holliday Tanner. *Doc Holliday: A Family Portrait.* University of Oklahoma Press. (P)

C. Tefertiller. *Wyatt Earp: The Life Behind the Legend.* John Wiley. (P)

Bob Boze Bell. *The Illustrated Life and Times of Doc Holliday.* Tri- Star Boze Publications. (P)

—. *The Illustrated Life and Times of Wyatt Earp.* Tri-Star Boze. (P)

Richard W. Etulain & Glenda Riley (eds.). *With Badges & Bullets: Lawmen and Outlaws in the Old West.* Fulcrum. (P)

CHAPTER 7: BANDITS AND BADMEN

Robertus Love. *The Rise and Fall Of Jesse James.* University of Nebraska Press. (P)

James D. Horan. *Desperate Men.* University of Nebraska Press. (P)

William A. Settle, Jr. *Jesse James Was His Name.* University of Missouri Press. (P)

T. J. Stiles. *Jesse James: Last Rebel of the Civil War.* Knopf. (H)

Cole Younger. *The Story of Cole Younger, by Himself.* Minnesota Hist. Society Press. (P)

Robert Barr Smith. *Daltons! The Raid on Coffeyville.* Kansas. University of Oklahoma Press. (P)

Glenn Shirley. *Gunfight at Ingalls: Death of on Outlaw Town.* Barbed Wire Press. (H)

Bailey C. Haines. *Bill Doolin: Outlaw O. T.* University of Oklahoma Press. (P)

RECOMMENDED READING

CHAPTER 8: THE GENTLER SEX

Dee Brown. *The Gentle Tamers*. University of Nebraska Press. (P)

Isabella Lucy Bird. *A Lady's Life in the Rocky Mountains*. University of Oklahoma Press. (P)

James D. Horan. *Desperate Women*. University of Nebraska Press. (P)

Glenn Clairmonte. *Calamity Was the Name for Jane*. Sage, Denver. (C)

Glenn Shirley. *Belle Starr and Her Times*. University of Oklahoma Press. (P)

Marshall Sprague. *Massacre: The Tragedy at White River*. University of Nebraska Press. (P)

Susan Shelby Magoffin. *Down The Santa Fe Trail and into Mexico*. Yale University Press. (P)

CHAPTER 9: BURY MY HEART AT WOUNDED KNEE

Helen Hunt Jackson. *A Century of Dishonour*. University of Oklahoma Press. (P)

David Lavender. *Let Me Be Free: the Nez Percé Tragedy.* University of Oklahoma Press. (P)

Keith A. Murray. *The Modocs and Their War*. University of Oklahoma Press. (P)

Ralph K. Andrist. *The Long Death: The Last Days of the Plains* Indians. University of Oklahoma Press. (P)

S. Ambrose. *Crazy Horse and Custer*. New American Library NY. (P)

Mari Sandoz. *Cheyenne Autumn*. University of Nebraska Press. (P)

Nicholas Black Elk. *Black Elk Speaks*. University of Nebraska Press. (P)

Edwin Sweeney. *Cochise: Chiricahua Apache Chief*. Norman, University of Oklahoma Press. (P)

Charles Robinson III. *General Crook and the Western Frontier*. University of Oklahoma Press. (H)

CHAPTER 10: THE LAST FRONTIER

A.S. Mercer. *The Banditti of the Plains, Or the Cattlemen's Invasion of Wyoming in 1892.* University of Oklahoma Press. (P)

Helena Huntington Smith. *The War on Powder River.* University of Nebraska Press. (P)

J. Evetts Haley. *The XIT Ranch and the Early Days of the Llano Estacado.* University of Oklahoma Press. (P)

Anne Meadows. *Digging Up Butch and Sundance.* University of Nebraska Press. (P)

Richard Patterson. *Butch Cassidy: A Biography.* University of Nebraska Press. (P)

Lula Parker Betenson. *Butch Cassidy My Brother.* Brigham Young University Press. (H)

Donna B. Ernst. *Sundance, My Uncle.* College Station, Texas: Creative Publishing. (H)

Glenda Riley & Richard W. Etulain. *By Grit & Grace: Eleven Women Who Shaped the American West.* Fulcrum (P)

OTHER GENERAL HISTORIES

Dan L. Thrapp. *Encyclopedia of Frontier Biography.* 4 vols. University of Nebraska Press. (P)

William C. Davis. *The American Frontier: Pioneers, Settlers and Cowboys, 1800–1899.* University of Oklahoma Press. (P)

Dee Brown. *Bury My Heart at Wounded Knee: An Indian History of the West.* Holt NY. (P)

——. & Martin F Schmitt. *Trail Driving Days.* Bonanza NY. (P)

——. *Fighting Indians of the West.* Bonanza NY. (P)

Joseph G. Rosa. *The Age of the Gunfighter.* University of Oklahoma Press. (P)

Eugene Cunningham. *Triggernometry: A Gallery of Gunfighters.* University of Oklahoma Press. (P)

Howard Lamar. *Encyclopedia of the West.* Crowell. (H)

Geoffrey C. Ward. *The West.* Little Brown, Boston. (H)

RECOMMENDED READING

INTERNET RESOURCES

A great deal of information on battlefields, State and National Parks and monuments can be accessed by searching for such locations as 'Little Big Horn,' 'The Alamo' or 'Sand Creek' and towns such as Dodge City, Deadwood and Tombstone or by using names like 'Jesse James' or 'Geronimo.' The following are links to some of the many sites featuring the history of the Old West and associated topics:

www.abebooks.com

www.truewestmagazine.com

www.thehistorynet.com

www.gunsoftheoldwest.com

www.cowboysindians.com

www.chronicleoftheoldwest.com

www.americancowboy.com

www.rangemagazine.com

www.shootmagazine.com

www.wildestwesterns.com

www.webdots.com/nola

www.HistoricTraveler.com

www.historyamerica.com

INDEX

INDEX

INDEX